Genetics Me... ...s Central Nervous Syste... ...pheral

STUDY GUIDE

Joyce Bishop
Golden West College
Huntington Beach, California

UNDERSTANDING
PSYCHOLOGY
THIRD EDITION

CHARLES G. MORRIS

University of Michigan

PRENTICE HALL
Upper Saddle River, New Jersey 07458

© 1996 by PRENTICE-HALL, INC.
Simon & Schuster / A Viacom Company
Upper Saddle River, New Jersey 07458

10 9 8 7 6 5 4 3 2 1

ISBN 0-13-443508-7
Printed in the United States of America

TABLE OF CONTENTS

HOW TO USE
THIS STUDY GUIDE

PREFACE

Your Time Is Valuable

Invest your study time so you get the greatest benefit!

The following techniques have been shown to increase a student's mastery of new information:

- Use as many of your senses and abilities as possible—writing, reading, hearing, speaking, drawing, etc.

- Organize information so it is meaningful to you.

- Study with other people whenever possible.

- Have FUN. We remember what we enjoy.

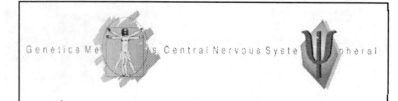

Genetics Me ... s Central Nervous Syste ... heral

1

Class and Text Notes

This section is designed so you can take notes on these pages during lecture and also from your reading of the text. Most students find it useful to read the text and make notes before the instructor covers the material in class.

Before you begin filling out this section decide how you will tell the difference between:

- your ideas
- lecture notes
- concepts from the text
- topics emphasized on the exam

Multiple Choice Pretest/Posttest

Practice exams are an important way to check your progress. The Pretest measures your starting point and the Posttest measures how far you have progressed toward your goal of mastering the material.

Short Essay Questions

Many college courses are designed to help you develop your writing skills so completing short essay questions can be useful. This is especially true if your psychology course will include essay exams.

Learning Objectives

After you have read and studied each chapter, you should be able to complete the learning objectives. Your exams are written based on the learning objectives so it is important to practice writing them.

Language Support

The *Language Support* section contains words students have identified from the text as needing more explanation. This section is for anyone who can benefit from extra support in English.

This page can be cut-out, folded in half, and used as a bookmark in the appropriate chapter.

During times of stress, flash cards can serve a very useful function. Stress is much worse when we feel over-whelmed; in fact, we tend to shut down and do nothing. At those times divide up what you have to do and do a small portion every day. Studying 10 flash cards today is less overwhelming than thinking about the 100 pages on your next exam.

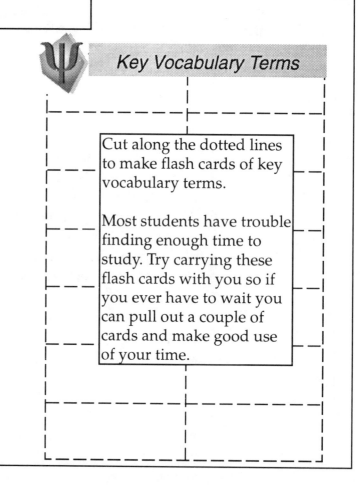

Key Vocabulary Terms

Cut along the dotted lines to make flash cards of key vocabulary terms.

Most students have trouble finding enough time to study. Try carrying these flash cards with you so if you ever have to wait you can pull out a couple of cards and make good use of your time.

STUDY TIPS

Improving Your Memory

1. Learn general first and then specific.

2. Make material meaningful to you.

3. Create associations with what you already know.

4. Learn it actively.

5. Imagine vivid pictures.

6. Recite out loud.

7. Reduce noise and interruptions.

8. Overlearn the material.

9. Be aware of your attitude toward information.

10. Space out learning over several days.

11. Remember related information when you are having trouble recalling something.

12. Use mnemonic devices (rhymes or words created from material).

13. Combine several of these techniques at once.

Memorizing Complex Information

There are memory techniques that make learning easier and faster. One technique, known as the "loci memory system", involves picturing yourself in a familiar setting and associating it with something you need to learn. Let's assume that you needed to memorize the function and structure of a neuron. Begin by picturing yourself walking into the entry hall of your home. At the same time pretend that you are walking through a dendrite. As you walk down the hall toward the living room, imagine that you are traveling in the dendrite to the cell body. As you exit the living room and walk down the hall toward the bedrooms, think of traveling down an axon toward the terminal button that contains the neurotransmitter. In this example you are connecting new information with something very familiar. We recall information much better when we involve our imagination. An even better way to perform this exercise would be to actually walk through your home while you visualize the parts of a neuron. In this situation you would not only be using your imagination but at the same time doing something physically. It is important to realize that we have strong memories for what we do physically. Just think how long you have remembered how to ride a bike even though you may not have ridden a bike for years.

When and How to study

1. Plan two hours study time for every hour you spend in class.
2. Study difficult or boring subjects first.
3. Avoid long study sessions.
4. Be aware of your best time of day.
5. Use waiting time by studying flash cards.
6. Use a regular study area.
7. Don't get too comfortable.
8. Use a library.
9. Take frequent breaks.
10. Avoid noise distractions.

Study in Groups

Research has shown that one of the most effective ways to learn is to study with other students. Your grades on exams will be better and you will have a lot more fun doing it!

How to form a group

1. Look for dedicated students who share some of your academic goals and challenges.

2. You could write a note on the blackboard asking interested students to contact you, or pass around a sign-up sheet before class.

3. Limit groups to five or six people.

4. Test the group by planning a one-time-only session. If that session works, plan another.

Possible activities for a study group

1. Compare notes.

2. Have discussions and debates about the material.

3. Test each other with questions brought to the group meeting by each member.

4. Practice teaching each other.

5. Brainstorm possible test questions.

6. Share suggestions for problems in the areas of finances, transportation, child care, time scheduling, or other barriers.

7. Develop a plan at the beginning of each meeting from the list above or any ideas you have.

Better Test Taking

1. Predict the test questions. Ask your instructor to describe the test format—how long it will be, and what kind of questions to expect (essay, multiple choice, problems, etc.).
2. Have a section in your notebook labeled "Test Questions" and add several questions to this section after every lecture and after reading the text. Record topics that the instructor repeats several times or goes back to in subsequent lectures. Write down questions the instructor poses to students.
3. Arrive early so you can do a relaxation exercise.
4. Ask about procedure for asking questions during test.
5. Know the rules for taking the test so you do not create the impression of cheating.
6. Scan the whole test immediately. Budget your time based on how many points each section is worth.
7. Read the directions slowly. Then reread them.
8. Answer easiest, shortest questions first. This gives you the experience of success and stimulates associations. This prepares your mind for more difficult questions.
9. Next answer multiple-choice, true-false, and fill-in-the-blank questions.
10. Use memory techniques when you're stuck.
    - If your recall on something is blocked, remember something else that's related.
    - Start from the general and go to specific
11. Look for answers in other test questions. A term, name, date, or other fact that you can't remember might appear in the test itself.
12. Don't change an answer unless you are sure because your first instinct is usually best.

Tips on Test Taking

Multiple-choice questions
1. Check the directions to see if the questions call for more than one answer.
2. Answer each question in your head before you look at the possible answers, otherwise you may be confused by the choices.
3. Mark questions you can't answer immediately and come back to them if you have time.
4. If incorrect answers are not deducted from your score, use the following guidelines to guess:
   - If two answers are similar, except for one or two words, choose one of these answers.
   - If two answers have similar sounding or looking words, choose one of these answers.
   - If the answer calls for a sentence completion, eliminate the answers that would not form grammatically correct sentences.
   - If answers cover a numerical range, choose one in the middle.
   - If all else fails, close your eyes and pick one.

True-False Questions
1. Answer these questions quickly.
2. Don't invest a lot of time unless they are worth many points.
3. If any part of the true-false statement is false, the whole statement is false.
4. Absolute qualifiers such as "always" or "never" generally indicate a false statement.

Machine-Graded Tests
1. Check the test against the answer sheet often.
2. Watch for stray marks that look like answers.

Open-Book and Notes Tests
1. Write down key points on a separate sheet.
2. Tape flags onto important pages of the book.
3. Number your notes, write a table of contents.
4. Prepare thoroughly because they are usually the most difficult tests.

Essay questions
1. Find out precisely what the question is asking. Don't *explain* when asked to *compare*.
2. Make an outline before writing. (Mindmaps work well.)
3. Be brief, write clearly, use a pen, get to the point, and use examples.

Reading for Remembering

1. **Skim**
   Skim the entire chapter.
2. **Outline**
   Read the outline at the front of the chapter in the text.
3. **Questions**
   Write out several questions that come to your mind that you think will be answered in the chapter.
4. **Read** the material.
5. **Highlight**
   While reading highlight the most important information (no more than 10%).
6. **Answers**
   As you read, get the answers to your questions.
7. **Recite**
   When you finish reading an assignment, make a speech about it. Recite the key points.
8. **Review**
   Plan your first review within 24 hours.
9. **Review again**
   Weekly reviews are important–perhaps only four or five minutes per assignment. Go over your notes. Read the highlighted parts of your text. Recite the more complicated points.

More about review

You can do short reviews anytime, anywhere, if you are prepared. Take your text to the dentist's office, and if you don't have time to read a whole assignment, review last week's assignment. Conduct five minute reviews when you are waiting for water to boil. Three-by-five cards work well for review. Write ideas and facts on cards and carry them with you. These short review periods can be effortless and fun.

Anxiety interferes with Performance

Do you freeze up on exams, worry that you won't do well? We can turn one exam into a "do or die" catastrophic situation. Yes, we should try our best but we are not doomed for life if we fail at something. Perhaps the following examples will help you see a failure for what it is, just one more step in the process of life.

- Einstein was four years old before he could speak and seven before he could read.

- Isaac Newton did poorly in grade school.

- Beethoven's music teacher once said of him, "As a composer he is hopeless."

- When Thomas Edison was a boy, his teachers told him he was too stupid to learn anything.

- Woolworth got a job in a dry goods store when he was 21, but his employers would not let him wait on a customer because he "didn't have enough sense."

- A newspaper editor fired Walt Disney because he had "no good ideas".

- Leo Tolstoy flunked out of college.

- Louis Pasteur was rated as "mediocre" in chemistry when he attended college.

- Abraham Lincoln entered the Black Hawk War as a captain and came out as a private.

- Winston Churchill failed the sixth grade.

Effective Note-Taking During Class

1. **Review the textbook chapter before class.**
   Instructors often design a lecture based on the assumption that you have read the chapter before class. You can take notes more easily if you already have some idea of the material.
2. **Bring your favorite note-taking tools to class.**
   Make sure you have pencils, pens, highlighter, markers, paper, note cards, or whatever materials you find useful.
3. **Sit as close to the instructor as possible.**
   You will have fewer distractions while taking your notes.
4. **Arrive to class early.**
   Relax and get your brain "tuned-up" to the subject by reviewing your notes from the previous class.
5. **Picture yourself up front with the instructor.**
   The more connected you feel to the material and the instructor, the more you will understand and remember the topic.
6. **Let go of judgments and debates.**
   Focus on understanding what the instructor is saying because that is what you will find on the test. Do not get distracted by evaluating the instructor's lecture style, appearance or strange habits. When you hear something you disagree with, make a quick note of it and then let it go.
7. **Be active in class.**
   It is the best way to stay awake in class! Volunteer for demonstrations. Join in class discussions.
8. **Relate the topic to an interest of yours.**
   We remember things we are most interested in.
9. **Watch for clues of what is important.**
   * repetition
   * summary statements
   * information written on the board
   * information the instructor takes directly from his or her notes
   * notice what interests the instructor

When Instructors Talk Too Fast

1. Read the material before class.

2. Review notes with classmates.

3. Leave large empty spaces in your notes.

4. Have a symbol that indicates to you that you have missed something.

5. Write down key points only and revise your notes right after class to add details.

6. Choose to focus on what you believe to be key information.

7. See the instructor after class and fill in what you missed.

8. Ask the instructor to slow down if you think that is appropriate.

Neurons Endoc   tem Behavior

Overview

● ●

THE SCIENCE OF PSYCHOLOGY

1

Class and Text Notes

This outline provides a way to organize your notes from both the text and the lecture. It will also serve as review sheets for the exam.

The Field of Psychology

Developmental Psychology

Physiological Psychology

Experimental Psychology

Personality Psychology

Clinical and Counseling Psychology

Social Psychology

Industrial and Organizational Psychology

The Goals of Psychology

Research Methods in Psychology

    Naturalistic Observation

    Case Studies

    Surveys

    Correlational Research

    Experimental Research

    Multimethod Research

Issues of Gender, Race, and Culture in Research

    The Importance of Sampling

    Unintended Biases

Issues of Ethics in Psychology

Ethics in Research on Humans

Ethics in Research on Nonhuman Animals

The Growth of Psychology as a Science

Wilhelm Wundt and Edward Bradford Titchener: Structuralism

William James: Functionalism

Sigmund Freud: Psychodynamic Psychology

John B. Watson: Behaviorism

Gestalt Psychology

B.F. Skinner: Behaviorism Revisited

Existential and Humanistic Psychology

Cognitive Psychology

The Multiple Perspectives of Psychology Today

Careers in Psychology

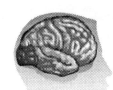

Multiple Choice Pretest

This pretest will help you identify the topics in the chapter that are most difficult for you. By focusing your study time in those areas, you will see the greatest improvement.

1. Psychologists who study how people change as they grow older are called _____ psychologists.
    a. social
    b. clinical
    c. developmental
    d. organizational

2. Psychologists who see patients in the hospital are called _____.
    a. clinical psychologists
    b. educational psychologists
    c. industrial psychologists
    d. developmental psychologists

3. Fifty percent of psychologists work in the area of
    a. personality or development.
    b. physiological or experimental.
    c. clinical or counseling.
    d. social or development.

4. The processes involved in learning, memory, sensation, perception, and cognition are investigated by _____ psychologists.
    a. organizational
    b. experimental
    c. educational
    d. social

5. Psychology is the study of behavior and _____.
    a. emotions
    b. functionalism
    c. mental processes
    d. structuralism

6. The _____ is composed formulating a hypothesis, careful observations, gathering data, and analyzing the data.
    a. scientific method
    b. introspection method
    c. deductive method
    d. inductive method

7. All of the following are goals of psychology EXCEPT
    a. reinforcement
    b. control
    c. prediction
    d. description

8. When you watch children play at a day care center to gather information about the difference in aggression between boys and girls, you are using the _____ research method.
    a. experimental
    b. case study
    c. correlational
    d. naturalistic observation

9. A research method that studies a person in-depth for some time through the use of observation, interviews, and writings is the _____ method.
    a. psychometric
    b. naturalistic observation
    c. survey
    d. case study

10. In _____ research people are asked a set of questions.
    a. correlational
    b. survey
    c. experimental
    d. analytical

11. People are sometimes given tests to predict their future performance in school or on the job. These tests are called _____ studies.
    a. case
    b. longitudinal
    c. correlational
    d. cross sectional

12. The _____ research method should be used if the cause of a behavior is to be determined.
    a. experimental
    b. longitudinal
    c. correlational
    d. cross sectional

13. In an experiment to test the effects of stress on performance, the independent variable is _____.
    a. performance
    b. age of the person
    c. stress
    d. test score

14. Which group does not receive the treatment and is used for comparison?
    a. independent
    b. dependent
    c. experimental
    d. control

15. Population is to _____ as sample is to
    _____.
    a. whole; part   c. part; whole
    b. research subjects   d. control subjects

16. Milgram's research focused on _____.
    a. learning   c. biofeedback
    b. obedience   d. pain thresholds

17. The first psychology lab was opened by
    _____.
    a. Watson   c. Wundt
    b. James   d. Freud

18. Structuralism emphasizes _____.
    a. the basic units of experience and their
       combinations
    b. the influence of the unconscious
    c. biological principles
    d. individual difference

19. Functionalism emphasizes that _____.
    a. research should be done through objective
       introspection
    b. individual differences are the basis of
       human behavior
    c. consciousness is a continuous flow
    d. consciousness is composed of three
       elements

20. Freud believed that our behavior is controlled
    by _____.
    a. environmental stimuli
    b. mental associations
    c. Gestalt interactions
    d. unconscious desires

21. Freud believed that unresolved conflicts
    during developmental stages may result in
    _____.
    a. fixation
    b. limited perception
    c. distortion
    d. an inferiority complex

22. Behaviorism was founded by _____.
    a. James   c. Titchener
    b. Watson   d. Wundt

23. _____ psychologists are concerned with
    the scientific study of mental processes.
    a. Humanistic   c. Cognitive
    b. Existential   d. Behavioral

Answers and Explanations to Multiple Choice Pretest

1. c. Developmental psychology focuses on how people change as they age.

2. a. Clinical psychologists see patients in the hospital and private clinics.

3. c. 50% of all psychologists work in the areas of clinical and counseling psychology.

4. b. Experimental psychologists study our perceptions, behaviors, and emotions.

5. c. The field of psychology studies behavior and mental processes.

6. a. The scientific method provides an excellent way to obtain and analyze data.

7. a. Goals of psychology are to describe, predict, and control behavior.

8. d. Naturalistic observation involves observing a person's or an animal's behavior without interfering.

9. d. In the case study method a person is studied in great depth.

10. b. The survey method can utilize either questionnaires or face-to-face interviews.

11. c. Correlational studies can only show that two things are associated.

12. a. Experimental method is able to show cause and effect.

13. c. Stress is the independent variable.

14. d. The control group is important for comparison to the experimental group.

15. a. Analogy: population is the whole group of people of interest, and the sample is a small part of the population.

16. b. Milgram studied obedience.

17. c. Wundt opened the first psychology lab.

18. a. Structuralism emphasizes basic units of experience and their combinations.

19. c. Functionalism emphasizes that consciousness is a continuous flow.

20. d. Freud believed our unconscious thoughts were very important.

21. a. Freud believed that unresolved conflict resulted in fixation at a specific psychosexual stage.

22. b. Watson founded behaviorism.

23. c. Cognitive psychologists emphasize mental processes.

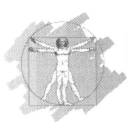

Learning Objectives

After you have read and studied this chapter, you should be able to complete the following statements. Your exam is written based on these learning objectives.

1. Describe the major fields of psychology including developmental, physiological, experimental, personality, clinical and counseling, social, and industrial/organization psychology.

2. Summarize the goals of psychology.

3. Distinguish between the five basic methods used by psychologists to gather information about behavior. Identify the situations in which each of the methods would be appropriate.

4. Describe the importance of sampling related to issues of gender, race, and culture in research.

5. Discuss the concerns of ethics in psychology.

6. Describe the early schools of psychology and explain how they contributed to its development.

7. Explain the difference between psychiatrists, psychologists, and psychoanalysts.

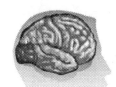

Short Essay Questions

Write out your answers to the following eight essay questions to further your mastery of the topics.

1. Explain what case studies are and how they are useful. What are the major advantages and disadvantages of this type of research?

_____

_____

_____

_____

_____

_____

_____

_____

_____

_____

_____

_____

2. Discuss samples and populations. What can a researcher do to overcome obstacles to obtaining a good sample?

_____

_____

_____

_____

_____

_____

_____

_____

_____

_____

3. Explain correlational research. What are the advantages and disadvantages of this type of research?

_____

_____

_____

_____

_____

_____

_____

_____

_____

_____

_____

_____

4. Explain Milgram's research and why it was so controversial. _____

_____

_____

_____

_____

_____

_____

_____

_____

_____

_____

5. Describe six basic principles from APA's 1992 ethics guidelines for researchers.

_____

_____

_____

_____

_____

_____

_____

_____

_____

_____

_____

6. Describe the differences between the structuralist and functionalist schools of psychology.

_____

_____

_____

_____

_____

_____

_____

_____

_____

_____

_____

7. Compare and contrast behaviorism and cognitive psychology.

_____

_____

_____

_____

_____

_____

_____

_____

_____

_____

_____

_____

_____

8. Explain Freud's psychoanalytic theory.

_____

_____

_____

_____

_____

_____

_____

_____

_____

_____

_____

_____

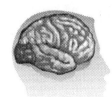

Language Support

Students identified the following words from the text as needing more explanation. This page can be cut-out, folded in half, and used as a bookmark for this chapter.

A
accurately	correctly
adopted	began to believe in
adverse affects	bad affects
amid	with
anticipatory	to do before something occurs
aptitude	ability
artificial	not real
assumptions	beliefs
automation	machine does the work instead of people

B
branch out	get more diverse training
broad field	wide areas
bystanders	people standing off to the side

C
candidate	someone running for political office
capacity	ability
cautious	careful
commonsense assumptions	ideas that seem reasonable
comprehensive	including many things
conduct	run
conform	to along with
conscientiousness	doing most things very carefully
constitute	make up
constraints	rules
contemporary	current, modern
context	in the situation; environment
controversy	differing opinion
curious	interested in

D
deception	not tell the truth
deficits	problems
disguised form	hidden shape
dissertation	research paper done to complete doctoral degree

E
embedded	hidden in
emerged	come out
endangered species	type of animals that may not live any more
ensure	make sure
established	shown
examines	looks at, studies
exhausted	to use up
explicitly	specifically
explore	look around
exploring	looking at

extent	amount

G-H-I

grappled	struggled
huge	large, big
impartial	not biased
impose	put
in the wake of	after
incidence	rate they occur
incidentally	by the way
influenced	changed
inhumane	very mean treatment

J-K-L-M

jargon	wording that is hard to understand
kept tabs on	studied over time
loopholes	problems
manipulate	control
methodological reasoning	scientific thinking
minimize	think something is less important than it really is
morale	feelings about their work

O-P

optimists	someone who sees the good side of most things
outgoing	friendly and not shy
outset	at the beginning
participate	take part of
pessimists	someone who sees the bad side of most things
phenomenon	occurrences
practical	useful
predominated	been the most important
prejudice	change falsely
proximity	being close
pursue	go after

R-S

receptive audience	very interested people
reevaluate	look at again
screening	picking carefully
short life spans	live only a very few years
shortcomings	problems
skeptical	do not believe
societal prohibitions	cultural rules against
stringent	strict
stuffy nose	cannot breath through nose due to cold or allergy
subjectively biased	done to our own benefit
subliminal messages	information given but people are not aware of it
suburban	small cities lying outside of big cities
superb	excellent
temperaments	personality types
thinly disguised	hidden but only a little
to abide by	to follow
unambiguous	clear
unanimous	all in agreement
underlying	basic
unequivocal	certain

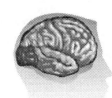

Multiple Choice Posttest

After studying the text and completing the Study Guide activities, answer these questions to determine if you need to review any areas before the course exam.

1. Researchers have found that Schizophrenia is related to excesses of dopamine chemical in the brain. These researchers would likely be _____ psychologists.
    a. clinical
    b. psychoanalytical
    c. developmental
    d. physiological

2. _____ psychologists work to improve efficiency of people in business.
    a. Cognitive
    b. Developmental
    c. Industrial/organizational
    d. Physiological

3. Psychology is the science of _____.
    a. behavior and mental processes
    b. objective introspection
    c. inductive reasoning
    d. emotions

4. When studying a particular behavior, a psychologist first _____ it.
    a. describes
    b. explains
    c. controls
    d. predicts

5. A hypothesis is _____.
    a. the independent variable
    b. an explanation of a phenomenon
    c. a testable prediction derived from a theory
    d. the dependent variable

6. Research which observed behavior in its actual setting without controlling anything is called _____.
    a. correlational method
    b. naturalistic observation
    c. survey research
    d. psychometric study

7. The research method used by Freud was _____.
    a. correlational method
    b. naturalistic observation
    c. survey research
    d. case study method

8. The amount of association between two or more variables is _____.
    a. correlation
    b. naturalistic observation
    c. reliability
    d. synchronosity

9. The only research method that can demonstrate a cause and effect relationship between variables is the _____ method.
    a. correlational
    b. naturalistic observation
    c. survey research
    d. experimental

10. A researcher manipulates the _____ variable.
    a. placebo
    b. independent
    c. dependent
    d. correlational

11. Expectations by the experimenter that may have an effect on the results of an experiment are called _____.
    a. sample bias
    b. double-blind
    c. experimenter bias
    d. treatment bias

12. Population is to sample as _____ is to part.
    a. placebo
    b. independent variable
    c. dependent variable
    d. whole

13. It is important that a sample be _____ of the population.
    a. controlled
    b. biased
    c. representative
    d. independent

14. Subjects in Milgram's studies were TOLD they were taking part in studies on _____.
    a. obedience
    b. emotional deprivation
    c. public humiliation
    d. learning

15. Wundt learned to do _____.
    a. free association
    b. objective introspection
    c. subjective introspection
    d. psychoanalysis

16. The basic units of experience and their combinations were the foundation of _____.
    a. functionalism
    b. structuralism
    c. Gestalt
    d. behaviorism

17. Consciousness as a continuous flow is an important concept to _____.
    a. structuralism
    b. functionalism
    c. objective introspection
    d. behaviorism

18. Freud believed that adult problems usually _____.
    a. result in Freudian slips
    b. result in bad dreams
    c. can be traced back to critical stages during childhood
    d. are the result of poor behaviors

19. _____ believed that a child must overcome a sense of inferiority.
    a. Adler
    b. Freud
    c. Jung
    d. Maslow

20. Gestalt theory emphasizes _____.
    a. a flow of consciousness
    b. the atoms of thought
    c. environmental stimuli
    d. our tendency to see patterns

Answers and Explanations to Multiple Choice Posttest

1. d. Physiological psychology studies the chemistry of the brain.
2. c. Industrial/organization psychology work to make businesses more efficient.
3. a. Psychology is the science of behavior and mental processes.
4. a. The first goal of psychology is to describe behavior.
5. c. A hypothesis is a testable prediction.
6. b. Naturalistic observation involves watching a research subject in the natural setting.
7. d. Freud's research and theory were build upon case studies.
8. a. Correlational research can predict the amount of association between two or more variables.
9. d. Only the experimental method can show cause and effect.
10. b. A researcher manipulates the independent variable.
11. c. Experimenter bias can be caused by the expectations of the researcher.
12. d. Analogy: Population is to sample as whole is to part.
13. c. A sample is representative of the population when it contains the same proportion of various diverse groups.
14. d. Milgram subjects were told the research was about learning, but this was not true.
15. b. Wundt learn to do objective introspection.
16. b. Structuralism focuses on basic units of experiences and their combinations.
17. b. Consciousness as a continuous flow is important to functionalism.
18. c. Freud believed that a child's first five years are critically important to adult development.
19. a. Adler believed a child must overcome a sense of inferiority to develop normally.
20. d. Gestalt theory emphasizes our tendency to see patterns.

Key Vocabulary Terms

Cut-out each term and use as study cards.
Definition is on the backside of each term.

Psychology	Correlational method
Scientific method	Correlation
Theory	Subjects
Hypotheses	Independent variable
Naturalistic observation	Dependent variable
Case study	Experimental group
Surveys	Control group

Research technique based on the naturally occurring relationship between two or more variables.	The scientific study of behavior and mental processes.
Relationship between two or more variables.	An approach to knowledge characterized by collecting data, generating a theory that attempts to explain the data, producing testable hypotheses based on the theory , and testing those hypotheses empirically.
Individual whose reactions or responses are observed in an experiment.	Systematic explanation of a phenomenon; it organizes known facts, allows the prediction of new facts, and permits a degree of control over the phenomenon.
In an experiment, the variable that is manipulated to test its effects on the other, dependent variables.	Specific, testable predictions derived from a theory.
In an experiment, the variable that is measured to see how it is changed by manipulations in the independent variable.	Research method involving the systematic study of animal or human behavior in natural settings rather than in the laboratory.
In a controlled experiment the group subjected to a change in the independent variable.	Intensive description and analysis of single individual or a few individuals.
In a controlled experiment, the group not subjected to a change in the independent variable; used for comparison with the experimental group.	Questionnaire or interviews administered to a select group of people.

Experimenter bias	Behaviorism
Sample	Gestalt psychology
Random sample	Reinforcement
Representative sample	Existential psychology
Biased sample	Humanistic psychology
Structuralism	Cognitive psychology
Functionalist theory	Evolutionary psychology

School of psychology that studies only observable and measurable behavior.	Expectation by the experimenter that might influence the results of an experiment or their interpretation.
School of psychology that studies how people perceive and experience objects as whole patterns.	Selection of cases from a larger population
Anything that follows a response and makes that response more likely to recur.	Sample in which each potential subject has an equal chance of being selected.
School of psychology that sees the meaninglessness and alienation of modern life as leading to apathy and psychological problems.	Sample carefully chosen so that the characteristics of the subjects correspond closely to the characteristics of the larger population.
School of psychology that emphasizes nonverbal experience and altered states of consciousness as a means of realizing one's full human potential.	Sample that does not truly represent a whole population.
School of psychology devoted to the study of mental processes generally.	School of psychology that stresses the basic units of experience and the combinations in which they occur.
An approach and subfield of psychology concerned with the origins of behaviors and mental process, their adaptive value, and the purposes they continue to serve.	Theory of mental life and behavior that is concerned with how an organism uses its perceptual abilities to function in its environment.

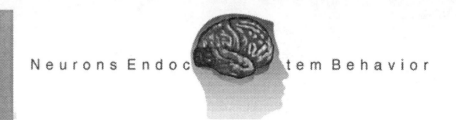

Neurons Endoctem Behavior

Overview

● ●

Neurons, the Messengers
The Neural Impulse
The Synapse
Synapses and Drugs

The Central Nervous System
The Brain
Hemispheric Specialization
New Tools for Studying the
     Nervous System
The Reticular Formation
The Limbic System
The Spinal Cord

The Peripheral Nervous System
The Somatic Nervous System
The Autonomic Nervous System

The Endocrine System
The Thyroid Gland
The Parathyroid Gland
The Pineal Gland
The Pancreas
The Pituitary Gland
The Gonads
The Adrenal Glands

Behavior Genetics
Genetics
Genetics and Behavior
Social Implications

PHYSIOLOGY AND BEHAVIOR

2

Class and Text Notes

This outline provides a way to organize your notes from both the text and the lecture. It will also serve as review sheets for the exam.

Neurons and the Neural Impulse

Dendrites

Cell body

Axon

Myelin sheath

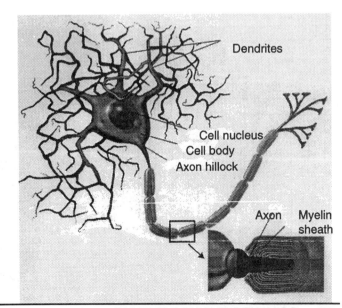

The Neural Impulse or Action Potential

Ions

Resting Potential

Polarization

Action Potential

Graded Potentials

Treshold of Excitation

Refractory Period

Relative Refractory Period

All-or-None Law

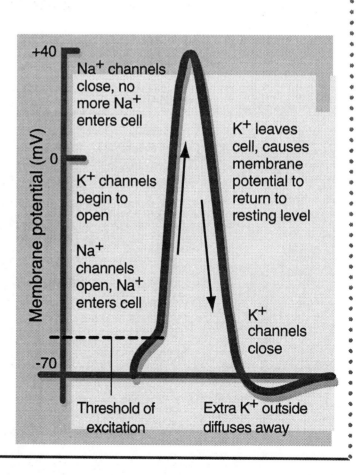

The Synapse

      Axon Terminal

      Synaptic Vesicles

      Synaptic Space

      Receptor Sites

Synapses and Drugs

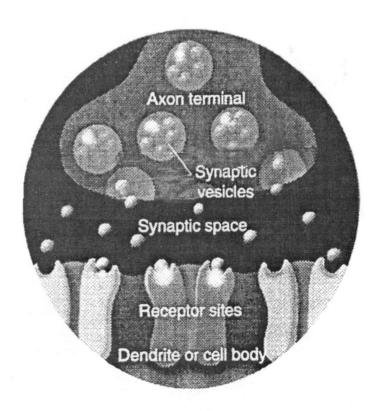

The Central Nervous System

The Brain

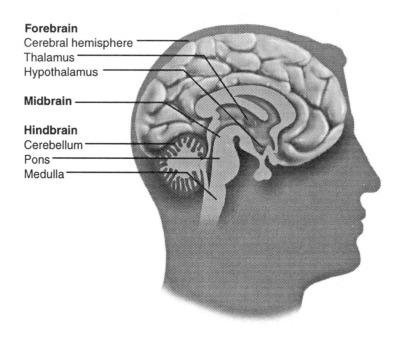

Forebrain
Cerebral hemisphere
Thalamus
Hypothalamus

Midbrain

Hindbrain
Cerebellum
Pons
Medulla

The Four Lobes of the Cerebral Cortex

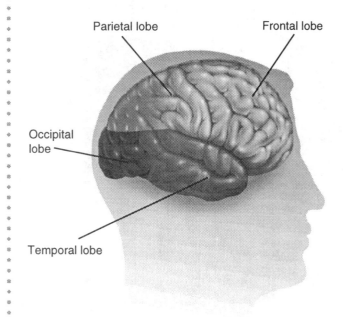

Parietal lobe

Frontal lobe

Occipital lobe

Temporal lobe

The Endocrine System

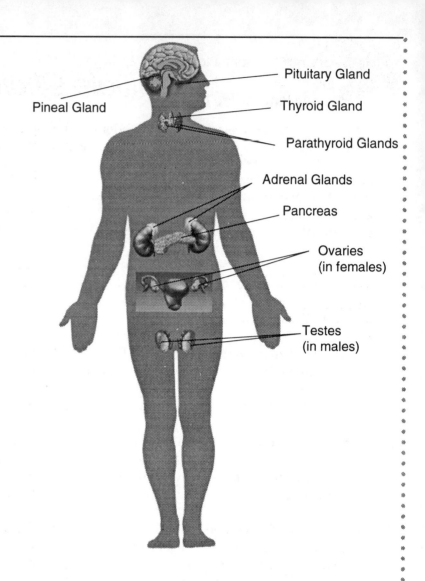

Pineal Gland

Pituitary Gland

Thyroid Gland

Parathyroid Glands

Adrenal Glands

Pancreas

Ovaries
(in females)

Testes
(in males)

The Thyroid Gland

The Parathyroid Gland

The Pineal Gland

The Pancreas

The Pituitary Gland

The Gonads

The Adrenal Glands

Behavior Genetics

Genetics

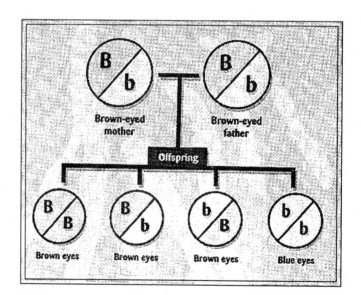

B / b
Brown-eyed
mother

B / b
Brown-eyed
father

Offspring

B / B
Brown eyes

B / b
Brown eyes

b / B
Brown eyes

b / b
Blue eyes

Genetics and Behavior

Social Implications

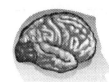

Multiple Choice Pretest

This pretest will help you identify the topics in the chapter that are most difficult for you. By focusing your study time in those areas, you will see the greatest improvement.

1. A single long fiber extending from the cell body that carries outgoing messages is called a/an
   a. dendrite.
   b. axon.
   c. nerve.
   d. terminal.

2. The primary purpose of the myelin sheath is to _____.
   a. provide a covering for the axon
   b. receive messages from outside the neuron and carry them to the cell nucleus
   c. insulate the neuron so the action potential is faster
   d. regulate neural respiration

3. Electrically charged particles are called _____.
   a. neurotransmitters
   b. electroparticles
   c. inhibitors
   d. ions

4. The time period after a neural impulse when the neuron can not fire again is called the
   a. relative refractory period.
   b. absolute refractory period.
   c. neural action potential.
   d. ionization state.

5. When the electrical charge inside a neuron is negative in relation to the outside, the neuron is said to be in a state of _____.
   a. depolarization
   b. polarization
   c. equilibrium
   d. shock

6. The _____ is composed of the axon terminal, the synaptic space, and the dendrite of the next neuron.
   a. synapse
   b. vesicle
   c. reception
   d. transmitter site

7. _____ is the chemical substance which is involved in the reduction of pain.
   a. Myelin
   b. Hormones
   c. Norepinephrine
   d. Endorphin

8. Breathing, heart rate, and blood pressure are controlled by the _____.
   a. medulla
   b. limbic system
   c. hypothalamus
   d. cerebral cortex

9. Analysis and problem solving are handled in the _____.
   a. thalamus
   b. hypothalamus
   c. cerebral cortex
   d. corpus callosum

10. What structure connects the two hemispheres of the brain and coordinates their activities?
    a. reticular formation
    b. amygdala
    c. hippocampus
    d. corpus callosum

11. The occipital lobe receives and interprets _____ information.
    a. auditory
    b. pain
    c. visual
    d. bodily position

12. The main function of the _____ is to alert and arouse the higher parts of the brain.
    a. limbic system
    b. reticular formation
    c. amygdala
    d. hippocampus

13. An injury to the _____ results in difficulty maintaining balance and coordinating movements.
    a. cerebellum
    b. medulla
    c. cerebral cortex
    d. hypothalamus

14. The rate of metabolism is controlled by the hormone _____.
    a. insulin
    b. thyroxin
    c. glycogens
    d. estrogen

15. Which nervous system is activated in an emergency?
    a. somatic
    b. sympathetic
    c. peripheral
    d. parasympathetic

16. The _____ regulates the stress response and is involved with emotional behavior.
    a. hypothalamus
    b. amygdala
    c. cerebellum
    d. medulla

17. The part of the brain that helps us focus on one thing and ignore distractions is the
    a. endocrine system.
    c. parietal lobe.
    b. reticular formation.
    d. temporal lobe.

18. _____ studies are used to examine the relative influence on behavior of heredity and the environment.
    a. Newton
    c. Twin
    b. Strain
    d. Stress

19. Behavior genetics is most concerned with
    a. studying the process of natural selection.
    b. controlling behavior through genetic manipulation.
    c. determining the influence of heredity on behavior.
    d. understanding how the environment can affect phenotype.

20. For many characteristics several genes work together in a process called _____.
    a. genetic dominance
    b. behavioral genetics
    c. natural selection
    d. polygenic inheritance

21. Which of the following have the most similar genetic composition?
    a. fraternal twins
    c. identical twins
    b. siblings
    d. cousins

22. Activity levels of the brain are examined using
    _____.
    a. PET-scans
    c. CT-scans
    b. NMR
    d. X-ray

23. All of the following show structure EXCEPT
    a. PET-scans.
    c. CT-scans.
    b. NMR.
    d. X-ray.

24. The brain scanning technique that offers the most hope for understanding disorders such as amnesia and dyslexia is _____.
    a. PET-scans
    c. CT-scans
    b. NMR
    d. MEG

25. Rhythmic variations in electrical activity are generated when a large number of neurons fire in the brain. These variations are called
    _____.
    a. oscillations
    c. biorhythms
    b. neural impulses
    d. brain waves

Answers and Explanations to Multiple Choice Pretest

1. b. The axon is a long fiber extending from the cells body that carries outgoing messages.

2. c. The myelin sheath insulates the axon and allows the neural impulse to "jump" and travel more quickly.

3. d. Ions are positive or negative particles.

4. b. Neurons can not fire during the absolute refractory period.

5. b. Polarization results when the electrical charge is different on the two sides of a membrane.

6. a. The axon terminal, the synaptic space, and the dendrite of the next neuron make up the synapse.

7. d. Endorphins are involved in the reduction of pain.

8. a. Breathing, heart rate, and blood pressure are controlled by the medulla.

9. c. Analysis and problem solving are handled in the cerebral cortex.

10. d. The corpus callosum connects the two hemispheres and coordinates their activities.

11. c. Visual information is process in occipital lobe.

12. b. The reticular formation arouses the brain.

13. a. The cerebellum coordinates movements and maintains balance.

14. b. Metabolism is controlled by thyroxin.

15. b. The sympathetic nervous system is active in an emergency.

16. a. The hypothalamus regulates the stress response and emotional behavior.

17. b. Reticular formation helps us to focus.

18. c. Twin studies are used to examine the influence of heredity and the environment on behavior.

19. c. Behavior genetics is most concerned with determining the influence of heredity on behavior.

20. d. Genes work together in a process called polygenic inheritance.

21. c. Identical twins are thought to have the most similar genetic information of any relative.

22. a. The PET-scan examines activity of the brain.

23. a. CT-scans, NMR, and X-Ray all show structure.

24. d. Magnetoencephalography (MEG) helps determine which parts of the brain are active for specific tasks.

25. d. Brain waves are rhythmic variations in electrical activity.

Learning Objectives

After you have read and studied this chapter, you should be able to complete the following statements. Your exam is written based on these learning objectives.

1. Describe the structure of neurons. Trace the path of a neural impulse and explain how it transmits messages from cell to cell.

2. Explain how neurons communicate. Identify the role of neurotransmitters and receptor. Describe the effect of drugs on the synapse.

3. Describe the divisions and structures of the brain and explain the roles of each.

4. Identify the functions of the sensory and motor projection areas. Describe the abilities of the two hemispheres of the cerebral cortex.

5. Describe the structure of and function of the reticular formation, limbic, system, and spinal cord.

6. Identify the division of the peripheral nervous system, and the autonomic nervous system and explain how they work together to regulate the glands and smooth muscles of the body.

7. Describe the functions of the endocrine system. Explain how hormones released by the endocrine system affect metabolism, blood-sugar level, sex characteristics, and the body's reaction to stress.

8. Summarize the concerns of behavior genetics.

9. Describe the structure of chromosomes and the role they play in inherited traits and characteristics.

10. Explain the concepts of dominant and recessive genes.

11. Identify several approaches to studying heritability of a trait.

12. Discuss some social implications of behavior genetics.

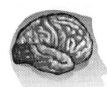

Short Essay Questions

Write out your answers to the following eight essay questions to further your mastery of the topics.

1. Explain how an action potential occurs and how a neuron returns to the resting state.

_____

_____

_____

_____

_____

_____

_____

_____

_____

_____

_____

_____

3. Compare and contrast the functions of the left and right hemispheres of the cerebral cortex.

_____

_____

_____

_____

_____

_____

_____

_____

_____

_____

_____

2. Explain how caffeine and cocaine impact neural communication and human behavior.

_____

_____

_____

_____

_____

_____

_____

_____

_____

_____

4. How do twin studies provide insights into environmental and genetic influences? _____

_____

_____

_____

_____

_____

_____

_____

_____

_____

_____

5. Describe the functions of the medulla, cerebellum, thalamus, hypothalamus, and cerebral cortex. _____

_____

_____

_____

_____

_____

_____

_____

_____

_____

_____

6. Compare the functions of the sympathetic and parasympathetic nervous system.

_____

_____

_____

_____

_____

_____

_____

_____

_____

_____

_____

7. Describe the functions of the frontal lobes, occipital lobes, temporal lobes, and parietal lobes.

_____

_____

_____

_____

_____

_____

_____

_____

_____

_____

_____

_____

8. Describe the uses and limitations of twin studies. _____

_____

_____

_____

_____

_____

_____

_____

_____

_____

_____

_____

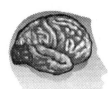

Language Support

Students identified the following words from the text as needing more explanation. This page can be cut-out, folded in half, and used as a bookmark for this chapter.

A
abnormalities	not normal
accumulate	build up
aftereffects	what happens afterwards
agitated	upset and nervous
anesthetic	chemical used so person does not feel pain
apathetic	do not care about anything
are literally	are really
arousal	being awake
attention span	how long a person can focus on something

B
bizarre	very strange
botulism	sickness caused by poison released by bacteria

C
composed of	made of
controversies	disagreement

D
deliberate	on purpose
devoted	only do one thing
diffuse randomly	move in every direction
disrupting	hurting
dominate	take control

E
ebullient	excited
energetic	a lot of energy
equilibrium	balance
especially important	very important
exaggerated	overstated
extraordinarily	exceptionally; very special

G
grooming	cleaning up our appearance
heated debate	intense discussion
hyperactivity	too much activity

I
imbalances	not the correct amount
immense	very large
impairment	problem
inbred	mate with close relative
incurable	can not make it better
insomnia	not being able to sleep
instantaneous	very fast
integrating	bring together
intricate	complex
intriguing	interesting

J
jerky motions	not smooth movement

L

leapfrog	a series of jumps
lethargy	fatigue; does not care about things

M

mallet	hammer
manual dexterity	ability to use hand well
merges	goes together
microorganism	bacteria or virus; germs
misperception	not the correct understanding

N

nonetheless	anyway; after all
numerous	many

O

occupy	stay in
orchestra	group of people playing musical instruments

P

paralysis	not being able to move
pioneers	first people
portions	part
predominate	is the main one
prescribed	given by a doctor
profound	very important
puzzled	confused

R

rage	very angry
reared	raised
reasoned	thought about
receptive	interested
recycled	used again
released	let go of
ribbonlike	flat band that is the shape of ribbon

S

scalp	skin covering head
severely	very
sluggish	slow
snap decisions	fast decisions; without thinking about it
spasms	fast muscles movements
spectacular	amazing
startling	very surprising
state of expectancy	waiting for something to happen
strenuously	intensely
suppressing	holding down
susceptibility	likely to get
systematically	step by step in an organized way

T

terror	very fearful
three-dimensional	objects with several sides
tremors	legs and arms shake
trigger	start
twitches	small, fast muscle movements

U

unprecedented	not seen before
uppercase letter	capital letter, such as "C"

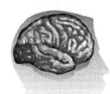

Multiple Choice Posttest

After studying the text and completing the Study Guide activities, answer these questions to determine if you need to review any areas before the course exam.

1. Short fibers that branch out from the cell body and pick up incoming messages are called
   a. dendrites.   c. nerves.
   b. axons.   d. terminals.

2. The metabolism of the neuron occurs in the _____.
   a. dendrites.   c. nerves.
   b. axons.   d. cell body.

3. Neurons that receive information from sensory organs and relay that information to the spinal cord and the brain are called _____.
   a. association neurons   c. afferent neurons
   b. efferent neurons   d. ions

4. When a neuron is polarized, _____.
   a. potassium ions pass freely through the cell membrane
   b. the electrical charge inside is positive relative to the outside
   c. it cannot fire
   d. the electrical charge inside is negative relative to the outside

5. If the stimulation of a neuron causes only a subthreshold change in electrical charge, the result is called _____.
   a. a graded potential   c. diffusion
   b. an action potential   d. a refraction

6. The "all or none" law refers to _____.
   a. a group of neurons fires together
   b. a neuron fires at full strength or not at all
   c. all the dendrites must be receiving messages telling the neuron to fire or it will not fire at all
   d. all the neurons in a single nerve fire simultaneously

7. A person with Parkinson's disease probably has a deficiency of _____.
   a. norepinephrine   c. dopamine
   b. serotonin   d. acetylcholine

8. Morphine and other opiates are able to bind to the receptor sites for _____.
   a. acetylcholine   c. dopamine
   b. hypothalamus   d. endorphins

9. Eating, drinking, sexual behavior, sleeping and temperature control are regulated by the _____.
   a. thalamus   c. cerebral cortex
   b. hypothalamus   d. corpus callosum

10. What structure connects the two hemispheres of the brain and coordinates their activities?
    a. reticular formation   c. hippocampus
    b. amygdala   d. corpus callosum

11. The temporal lobe receives and interprets _____ information.
    a. auditory   c. visual
    b. pain   d. bodily position

12. A part of the brain that sends the signal "Alert" to higher centers of the brain in response to incoming messages is _____.
    a. limbic system   c. amygdala
    b. reticular formation   d. hippocampus

13. An injury to the _____ results in difficulty with memory.
    a. cerebellum   c. cerebral cortex
    b. medulla   d. hippocampus

14. The thyroid gland controls _____.
    a. glucose absorption   c. metabolism
    b. emotions   d. sexuality

15. A car almost hit you as you were walking across the street. Which nervous system did this event probably activate in you?
    a. somatic   c. peripheral
    b. sympathetic   d. parasympathetic

16. Which hemisphere of the cerebral cortex is usually dominant in spatial tasks?
    a. frontal   c. lateral
    b. left   d. right

17. The limbic system is responsible for _____.
    a. controlling learning and emotional behavior
    b. providing a bridge for numerous brain areas
    c. analyzing problems situations
    d. fighting pathogens

18. Reflexes are usually controlled by the _____.
    a. frontal lobe   c. spinal cord
    b. medulla   d. hypothalamus

19. A person's genetic information is carried by
    a. acetylcholine   c. DNA
    b. thyroxin   d. NMR

20. _____ is a test on a fetus to determine if there are any genetic abnormalities.
    a. Amniocentesis
    b. Positron emission tomography
    c. Magnetic resonance
    d. CT - scans

21. What are the social implications of amniocentesis when abnormalities are found?
    a. Should society protect the unborn baby?
    b. Does a child with genetic abnormalities have a right to life?
    c. Which defects are so unacceptable that abortion is justified?
    d. All of the above are social considerations.

22. What technique would you use to determine if someone is having difficulty processing visual information?
    a. PET-scans   c. CT-scans
    b. NMR   d. X-ray

23. All of the following show activity EXCEPT
    a. PET.   c. EEG.
    b. MRI.   d. MEG.

24. The gonads produce the male sex hormones called _____.
    a. oxytocin   c. progesterone
    b. thyroxin   d. testosterone

25. Brain waves that are found when a person is relaxing are called _____.
    a. alpha waves   c. theta waves
    b. delta waves   d. deep waves

Answers and Explanations to Multiple Choice Posttest

1. a. Dendrites branch out from the cell body and pick up incoming messages.

2. d. The metabolism of the neuron occurs in the cell body.

3. c. Afferent neurons receive information from sensory organs and are also called sensory neurons.

4. d. Polarization is the result of unequal distribution of charged molecules across the membrane.

5. a. A graded potential is a change in polarization that is not large enough to reach threshold.

6. b. "All of none" refers to the principle that a neuron either fires at full strength or not at all.

7. c. A person with Parkinson's disease probably has a deficiency of dopamine.

8. d. Morphine can bind to the receptor sites for endorphins.

9. b. The hypothalamus regulates eating, drinking, sexual behavior, sleeping and temperature.

10. d. The corpus callosum connects the two hemispheres of the brain.

11. a. The temporal lobe receives auditory information.

12. b. The reticular formation gives the "alert" signal.

13. d. The hippocampus is important to memory.

14. c. The thyroid gland controls metabolism.

15. b. The sympathetic nervous system is activated when we experience fear.

16. d. Spatial tasks are usually handled in the right hemisphere.

17. a. The limbic system is responsible for controlling learning and emotional behavior.

18. c. The spinal cord controls most reflexes.

19. c. DNA contains our genetic information.

20. a. Amniocentesis involves extracting and examining genetic information.

21. d. All of the statements are considerations.

22. a. Only PET scans look at activity levels that would take place during processing.

23. b. MRI shows structure only.

24. d. Testosterone is the male hormone produced by the gonads.

25. a. Alpha waves are found when a person is relaxing.

Nervous system	Sensory or afferent neurons
Endocrine system	Motor or efferent neurons
Neurons	Interneurons
Dendrites	Glial cell
Axon	Ions
Nerve	Resting potential
Myelin sheath	Polarization

Neurons that carry messages from sense organs to the spinal cord or brain.	The brain, the spinal cord, and the network of nerve cells that transmit messages throughout the body.
Neurons that carry messages from the spinal cord or brain to the muscles and glands.	Internal network of glands that release hormones directly into the bloodstream to regulate body functions.
Neurons that carry messages from one neuron to another and do most of the work of the nervous system.	Individual cells that are the smallest unit of the nervous system.
Cell that forms the myelin sheath that insulates neurons and supports neurons by holding them together, removing waste products, and preventing harmful substances from passing from the bloodstream into the brain.	Short fibers that branch out from the cell body and pick up incoming messages.
Electrically charged particles found both inside and outside of the neuron.	Single long fiber extending from the cell body; it carries outgoing messages.
Electrical charge across a neuron membrane when sodium ions concentrate on the outside and potassium ions concentrate on the inside.	Groups of axons bundled together
The condition of a neuron when the inside is negatively charged relative to the outside; for example, when the neuron is at rest.	White fatty covering found on some axons.

Neural impulse or action potential	Synaptic space
Graded potential	Synapse
Threshold of excitation	Synaptic vesicles
Absolute refractory period	Neurotransmitters
Relative refractory period	Receptor site
All-or-none law	Central nervous system
Axon terminal	Peripheral nervous system

Tiny gap between the axon terminal of one neuron and the dendrites or cell body of the next neuron.	The firing of a nerve cell.
Area composed of the axon terminal of one neuron, the synaptic space, and the dendrite or cell body of the next neuron.	A shift in the electrical charge in a tiny area of a neuron.
Tiny sacs in a synaptic knob that release chemicals into the synapse.	The level an impulse must exceed to cause a neuron to fire.
Chemicals released by the synaptic vesicles that travel across the synaptic space and affect adjacent neurons.	A period after firing when a neuron will not fire again no matter how strong the incoming messages may be.
A location on a receptor neuron into which a specific neurotransmitter fits like a key into a lock.	A period after firing when a neuron is returning to its normal polarized state and will fire again only if the incoming message is much stronger than usual.
Division of the nervous system that consists or the brain and spinal cord.	Principle that the action potential in a neuron does not vary in strength; the neuron either fires at full strength or it does not fire at all.
Division of the nervous system that connects the central nervous system to the rest of the body.	Knob at the end of an axon terminal branch.

Medulla	Hypothalamus
Pons	Cerebral cortex
Cerebellum	Association areas
Brain stem	Occipital lobe
Midbrain	Temporal lobe
Forebrain	Parietal lobe
Thalamus	Sensory projection areas

Forebrain region that governs motivation and emotional responses.	Part of the hindbrain that controls such functions as breathing, heart rate, and blood pressure.
The outer surface of the two cerebral hemispheres that regulate most complex behavior.	Part of the hindbrain that connects the cerebral cortex at the top of the brain to the cerebellum.
Areas of the cerebral cortex where incoming messages from separate senses are combined into meaningful impressions and outgoing messages from the motor areas are integrated.	Two hemispheres in the hindbrain that control certain reflexes and coordinate the body's movements.
Part of the cerebral hemisphere that receives and interprets visual information.	The top of the spinal column; it widens out to form the hindbrain and midbrain.
Part of the cerebral hemisphere that helps regulate hearing, smell, balance and equilibrium, and certain emotions and motivations.	Region between the hindbrain and the forebrain; it is important for hearing and sight, and it is one of several places in the brain where pain is registered.
Part of the cerebral cortex that responds primarily to sensations of touch and bodily position.	Top part of the brain, including the thalamus, hypothalamus, and cerebral cortex.
Areas of the parietal lobe where message from the sense receptors are registered.	Forebrain region that relays and translates incoming messages from the sense receptors, except for those for smell.

Corpus callosum	Parasympathetic division
Reticular formation	Hormones
Limbic system	Endocrine glands
Spinal cord	Thyroid gland
Somatic nervous system	Thyroxin
Autonomic nervous system	Parathyroids
Sympathetic division	Parathormone

Branch of the autonomic nervous system; it calms and relaxes the body.	Band of nerve fibers that connects the two cerebral hemispheres and coordinates their activities.
Chemical substances released by the endocrine glands; they help regulate bodily activities.	Network of neurons in the hindbrain, midbrain, and part of the forebrain whose primary function is to alert and arouse the higher parts of the brain.
Glands of the endocrine system that release hormones into the bloodstream.	Ring of structures around the brain stem; it plays a role in learning and emotional behavior.
Endocrine gland located below the voice box; it produces the hormone thyroxin.	Complex cable of neurons that runs down the spine, connecting the brain to most of the rest of the body.
Hormone that regulates the body's rate of metabolism.	The part of the peripheral nervous system that carries messages from the senses to the central nervous system and between the central nervous system and the skeletal muscles.
Four tiny glands embedded in the thyroid; they secrete parathormone.	The part of the peripheral nervous system that carries messages between the central nervous system and the internal organs.
Hormone that controls the levels of calcium and phosphate in the blood and tissue fluids.	Branch of the autonomic nervous system, it prepares the body for quick action in an emergency.

Pancreas	Genetics
Pituitary gland	Genes
Adrenal glands	Chromosomes
Beta endorphin	Deoxyribonucleic acid (DNA)
ACTH	Polygenic inheritance
Behavior genetics	Twin studies
Heredity	Amniocentesis

Study of how traits are passed from one generation to the next.	Organ lying between the stomach and small intestine; it secretes insulin and glucagon.
Elements that control the transmission of traits; they are found on the chromosomes.	Gland located on the underside of the brain; it produces the largest number of the body's hormones.
Pairs of threadlike bodies within the cell nucleus that contain the genes.	Two endocrine glands located just above the kidneys.
Complex molecule that is the main ingredient of chromosomes and genes and forms the code for all genetic information.	One of the endorphins, a natural pain-killer released by the body.
Process in which several genes interact to produce a certain trait; responsible for our most important traits.	Hormone released by the anterior pituitary; it stimulates hormone production of the adrenal cortex.
Studies of identical and fraternal twins to determine the relative influence of heredity and environment on human behavior.	Study of the relationship between heredity and behavior.
Technique that involves collecting cells cast off by the fetus into the fluid of the womb and testing them for genetic abnormalities.	The transmission of traits from one generation to the next.

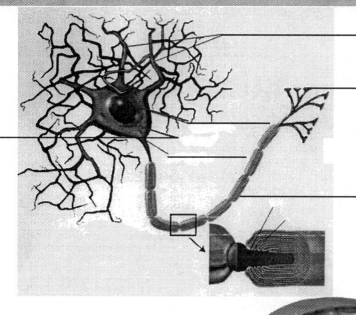

**Lobes of
the Brain**

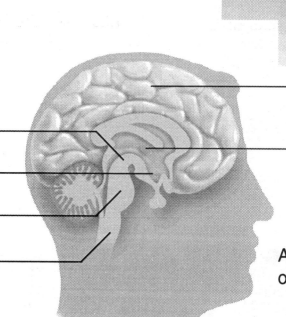

**A Cross Section
of the Brain**

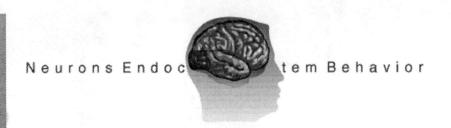

Overview

● ●

SENSATION AND PERCEPTION

3

Class and Text Notes

This outline provides a way to organize your notes from both the text and the lecture. It will also serve as review sheets for the exam.

The Nature of Sensory Processes

The General Character of Sensation

Sensory Thresholds

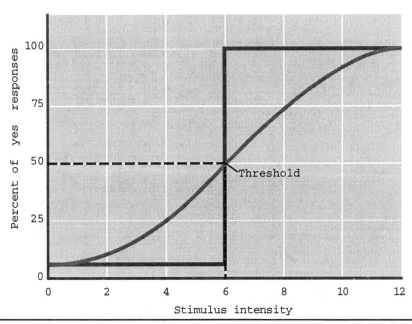

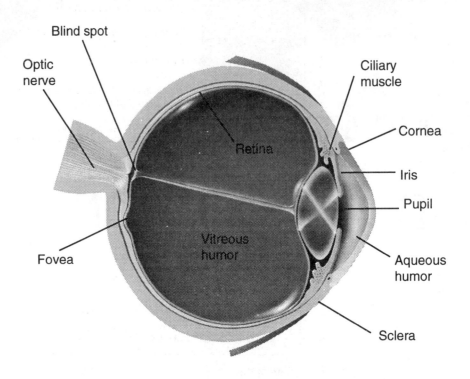

Blind spot

Optic
nerve

Ciliary
muscle

Cornea

Iris

Retina

Pupil

Fovea

Vitreous
humor

Aqueous
humor

Sclera

Color vision

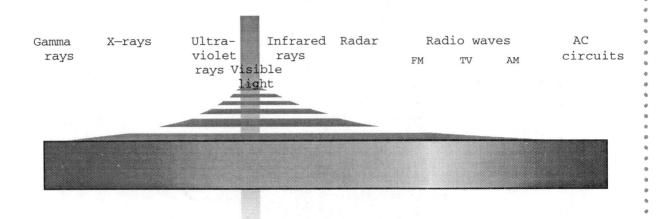

Gamma
rays

X—rays

Ultra-
violet
rays Visible
light

Infrared
rays

Radar

Radio waves

FM   TV   AM

AC
circuits

Hearing

Sound

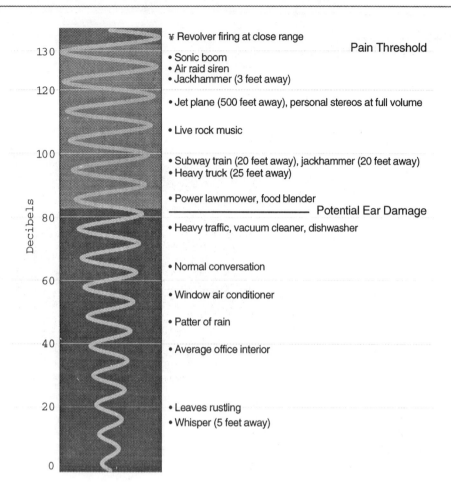

Decibels

130 — ¥ Revolver firing at close range   Pain Threshold
• Sonic boom
• Air raid siren
• Jackhammer (3 feet away)

120 — • Jet plane (500 feet away), personal stereos at full volume

• Live rock music

100 — • Subway train (20 feet away), jackhammer (20 feet away)
• Heavy truck (25 feet away)

• Power lawnmower, food blender
80 — ———————————————————— Potential Ear Damage
• Heavy traffic, vacuum cleaner, dishwasher

• Normal conversation
60 —
• Window air conditioner

• Patter of rain
40 —
• Average office interior

20 — • Leaves rustling
• Whisper (5 feet away)

0 —

The Ear

Theories of Hearing

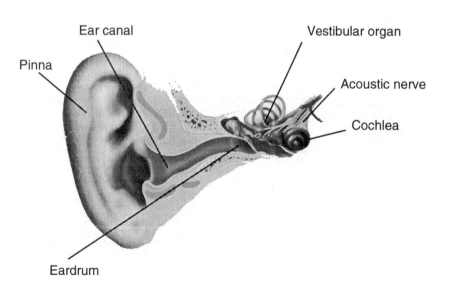

Ear canal

Vestibular organ

Pinna

Acoustic nerve

Cochlea

Eardrum

The Other Senses

Smell

Taste

Kinesthetic and Vestibular Senses

Sensations of Motion

The Skin Senses

Pain

Perception

Perceptual Organization

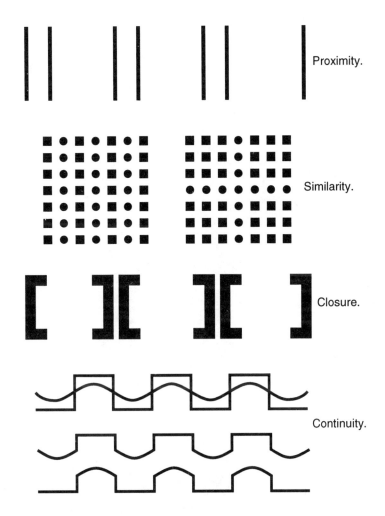

Proximity.

Similarity.

Closure.

Continuity.

Perceptual Constancies

Observer Characteristics

Perception of Distance and Depth

Perception of Movement

Visual Illusions

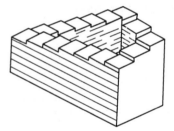 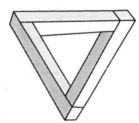 

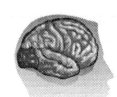

Multiple Choice Pretest

This pretest will help you identify the topics in the chapter that are most difficult for you. By focusing your study time in those areas, you will see the greatest improvement.

1. The process of sensation is _____.
    a. focused in the sympathetic nervous system
    b. the organization of stimuli into meaningful patterns
    c. the stimulation of the senses
    d. the internal activity in the absence of external stimulation

2. Creating meaningful patterns from sensory information is the process called _____.
    a. perception
    b. transduction
    c. motion parallax
    d. sensation

3. A receptor cell _____.
    a. responds to all intensities of stimulation
    b. responds to all types of energy
    c. can respond only to light energy
    d. is specialized to respond to one type of energy

4. When a stimulus can be detected 50 percent of the time it is called _____.
    a. noticeable threshold
    b. absolute threshold
    c. theoretical threshold
    d. difference threshold

5. A change in stimulation that can be detected 50% of the time is called _____.
    a. noticeable threshold
    b. absolute threshold
    c. theoretical threshold
    d. difference threshold

6. Messages that are supposedly sent to people which motivate them to buy a product without them being aware of the messages are called _____.
    a. subliminal messages
    b. selective perception
    c. inductive perception
    d. cognitive restructuring

7. Light enters the eye through the _____.
    a. fovea
    b. lens
    c. pupil
    d. retina

8. The colored part of the eye containing a muscle which changes the size of the pupil is the _____.
    a. fovea
    b. lens
    c. pupil
    d. iris

9. The _____ adjusts its shape in order to focus on different objects at different distances
    a. fovea
    b. lens
    c. pupil
    d. retina

10. What kinds of receptors are found in the retina?
    a. bipolar cells and cones
    b. ganglion cells and bipolar cells
    c. rods and cones
    d. rods and ganglion cells

11. Cones are _____.
    a. receptors for black and white
    b. found mainly in the fovea
    c. more sensitive to light than rods
    d. in operation mainly at night

12. Which of the following is NOT true of the blind spot?
    a. Even a bright light can not be seen from it.
    b. It is the part of the retina with the greatest visual acuity.
    c. It is the coming together of all ganglion cells.
    d. It contains no receptors.

13. When fluid builds up in the eye and causes damage to the optic nerve and then loss of vision, the disorder is called

    _____.
    a. myopia
    b. astigmatism
    c. prosopagnia
    d. glaucoma

14. Some researchers believe that a lack of coordination between messages sent from M-cells and those sent from P-cells in the retina, may, in part, be one of the factors causing _____.
    a. dyslexia   c. night blindness
    b. glaucoma   d. aphasia

15. Mixing lights of different wavelengths to create new hues such as on a computer monitor is called _____.
    a. subtractive color mixing
    b. trichromatic color mixing
    c. additive color mixing
    d. blending

16. Frequency determines _____.
    a. amplitude   c. overtones
    b. pitch   d. timbre

17. The height of a sound wave represents its _____.
    a. amplitude   c. overtones
    b. pitch   d. timbre

18. Decibels are used to measure_____.
    a. amplitude   c. overtones
    b. pitch   d. loudness

19. The hammer, anvil, and stirrup are the _____.
    a. components of the cochlea
    b. bones in the middle ear
    c. muscles in the oval window
    d. receptors in the inner ear

20. The cochlea is divided lengthwise by the _____.
    a. organ of Corti
    b. vestibular apparatus
    c. basilar membrane
    d. oval window

21. What are the two major pitch discrimination theories?
    a. frequency and amplitude theories
    b. transduction and volley theories
    c. place and amplitude theories
    d. place and frequency theories

Answers and Explanations to Multiple Choice Pretest

1. c. Sensation results from the stimulation of the senses.
2. a. Perception is creating meaningful patterns from sensations
3. d. Receptors are specialized to response to one type and some times also one intensity of energy.
4. b. Absolute threshold occurs when the stimulus is detected 50% of the time.
5. d. Difference threshold occurs when the difference between two stimuli is detected 50% of the time.
6. a. We are not aware of subliminal messages.
7. c. Light enters the eye through the pupil.
8. d. The colored part of the eye is the iris.
9. b. Lens adjust shape to focus at different objects at various distances.
10. c. Rods and cones are the receptors in the retina.
11. b. There are more cones in the fovea.
12. b. If an image lands on our blind spot we cannot see it.
13. d. Glaucoma results when excess fluid inside the eye causes high pressure.
14. a. Dyslexia may be lack of coordination between M-cells and P-cells.
15. c. Mixing sources of light is called additive color mixing.
16. b. Frequency of a sound wave results in our hearing a certain pitch of sound.
17. a. Height of a sound wave is the amplitude (loudness).
18. d. Loudness is measured in decibels.
19. b. Hammer, anvil, and stirrup are bones in the middle ear.
20. c. The cochlea is divided lengthwise by the basilar membrane.
21. d. Place and frequency theories explore how we hear pitch.

Learning Objectives

After you have read and studied this chapter, you should be able to complete the following statements. Your exam is written based on these learning objectives.

1. Describe the difference between the absolute threshold and the difference threshold.

2. Trace the path of light from the time it enters the eye until it reaches the receptor cells.

3. Distinguish between rods and cones, and list their characteristics and functions with respect to light, color, and how they connect to other cells.

4. Describe the process of adaptation, include the phenomenon of afterimages.

5. Explain how messages entering the eye are processed in the brain.

6. Describe the three basic properties of color. Distinguish between additive and subtractive color mixing.

7. Describe the two main theories of color vision.

8. Identify the characteristics of sound.

9. Describe the structure of the ear and explain the functions of the various parts.

10. State the two theories of pitch discrimination.

11. Describe hearing disorders.

12. Summarize the theories which explain how the sense of smell is activated by chemical substances.

13. Explain the processes involved in the sense of taste and name the four primary qualities of taste.

14. Explain the importance of vestibular senses and describe the functions of the two divisions.

15. Explain how the sensations of pressure, warmth, and cold originate and how people respond to them.

16. Describe three theories of pain.

17. Discuss the principles of perceptual organization identified by the Gestaltists.

18. Define perceptual constancy and identify four kinds.

19. Describe four observer characteristics which can affect perception.

20. Identify the contributions of both monocular and binocular cues of depth.

21. Explain real movement. Define and give three examples of apparent movement.

22. Describe two kinds of visual illusions.

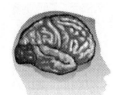

Short Essay Questions

Write out your answers to the following four essay questions to further your mastery of the topics.

1.   Compare and contrast sensation and perception. Also describe the events that produce a sensation.

_____

_____

_____

_____

_____

_____

_____

_____

_____

_____

_____

_____

2.   Define pitch, amplitude, decibels, overtones, and timbre.

_____

_____

_____

_____

_____

_____

_____

_____

_____

_____

_____

_____

3.   Differentiate between hue, brightness, and saturation. Explain the difference between additive and subtractive color mixing.

_____

_____

_____

_____

_____

_____

_____

_____

_____

_____

_____

_____

4.   Explain the causes for deafness and tinnitus.

_____

_____

_____

_____

_____

_____

_____

_____

_____

_____

_____

_____

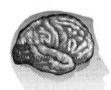

Language Support

Students identified the following words from the text as needing more explanation. This page can be cut-out, folded in half, and used as a bookmark for this chapter.

A
abundance   have many
adaptation   change to something
array   mixture
at a loss   cannot
B
"blip" on radar   small flash of light
blurred   not clear
booming   large
C
cast   fall
claws   nails on foot of animal
coherent   makes sense
contours   shape
D
deciphering   figuring out
depressed spot   spot is lower than the rest
destinations   place they go
detect   find
detected   found
deterioration   lose; decrease in ability
discriminate   tell the different between
disgusted   dislike a lot
distinct   special
distinguish   to tell the difference from
dull   not shiny
E
echoes   sound bouncing off something
effortlessly   to do easily
elderly people   older people (probably over 65 years old)
embedded   hidden in
exerted   done
exist   be
extraordinary   a very large
H
haze   cloudy
herd   group
hum   continuous sound
I
implants   devise put in
insensitive   not feel
intriguing   very interesting
L
leaf blowers   air machine that blows leaves instead of raking them up

N

negotiate traffic	go through traffic
nonhuman animals	animals, not including people
obstacles	problems
oversimplification	make it too easy

P-R

pedestrians	people walking by or on the street
perch	sit
permit us to	allow us to
precise	careful
precisely	exactly
preconceptions	ideas of what it is supposed to be
prism	glass that can divide light into colors
pups	baby animals

R

rapid tremor	fast movement back and forth
rate of firing	how many actions potentials in a certain amount of time
reflect	show
remarkable feat	to do a very difficult thing
rests	sits
route	path

S

self-esteem	how good or bad we feel about ourselves
solidity	being solid
sophisticated	very technical
squint	close eyes part of the way
stationary	not moving
synchronize	work together at the same time

T

taxing	difficult
tiny flick	very small movement

U

ultimate destinations	place in the very end

V

vice versa	the other way also

W

weakly	not strong
wearer	someone who wears
weight-loss tape	a cassette tape containing information to help someone loss weight

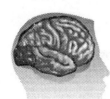

Multiple Choice Posttest

After studying the text and completing the Study Guide activities, answer these questions to determine if you need to review any areas before the course exam.

1. Sensation is to _____ as perception is to _____.
   a. stimulation; interpretation
   b. interpretation; stimulation
   c. sensory ability; sensory acuity
   d. sensory acuity; sensory ability

2. The _____ is reached when a person can detect a stimulus 50 percent of the time.
   a. difference threshold
   b. just noticeable threshold
   c. absolute threshold
   d. separation threshold

3. Which of the following is NOT true of subliminal perception?
   a. The effects attributed to subliminal perception may be the results of conscious expectations.
   b. Subliminal messages may be able to change attitudes.
   c. People can perceive stimuli they cannot consciously describe.
   d. It works equally as well in all people.

4. The clear, transparent, protective coating over the front part of the eye is the _____ .
   a. sclera   c. iris
   b. cornea   d. fovea

5. The lining inside the eye that contains the receptor cells is called the _____.
   a. cornea
   b. iris
   c. retina
   d. fovea

6. Receptors for light are called _____.
   a. rods and cones
   b. sclera and cornea
   c. iris and cornea
   d. iris and fovea

7. Which of the following is true about rods?
   a. They are responsible for night vision.
   b. They are found mainly in the fovea.
   c. They respond to color.
   d. They operate mainly in the daytime.

8. The ability of the eye to distinguish fine details is called _____.
   a. visual dilation
   b. visual acuity
   c. visual sensitivity
   d. adaptation

9. A disorder called _____ results when fluid pressure builds up inside the eye and cases damage to the optic nerve.
   a. prosopagnia
   b. achromatopsia
   c. dyslexia
   d. glaucoma

10. The process of mixing various pigments together to create different colors is called _____.
    a. blending
    b. trichromatic color mixing
    c. subtractive color mixing
    d. additive color mixing

11. Research suggests that _____.
    a. both the trichromatic and opponent-process theories of color vision are valid
    b. only the opponent-process theory is valid
    c. only the trichromatic theory is valid
    d. neither the opponent-process nor the trichromatic theory is valid

12. Pitch is _____.
    a. the timbre of a sound
    b. how high or low a sound is
    c. the overtones of a sound
    d. the amplitude of a sound wave

13. Hertz is a unit of measurement of _____.
    a. the timbre of a sound
    b. how high or low a sound is
    c. the frequency of a sound
    d. the amplitude of a sound wave

14. The snail-shaped structure in the inner ear is called the _____.
    a. basilar membrane
    b. stirrup
    c. auditory lobe
    d. cochlea

15. Flavor is _____.
    a. a combination of texture and taste
    b. a combination of taste and smell
    c. taste
    d. smell

16. The _____ has the most numerous receptors.
    a. skin
    b. eye
    c. ear
    d. nose

17. Optical illusions result from distortion in _____.
    a. transduction
    b. sensation
    c. perception
    d. adaptation

18. You know a house is the same size whether you are standing right next to it or a mile away from it because of _____.
    a. the phi phenomenon
    b. the figure-ground distinction
    c. retinal disparity
    d. perceptual constancy

19. Our general method for dealing with the environment is known as _____.
    a. intelligence
    b. perceptual style
    c. personality
    d. cognitive style

20. Visual distance and depth cues that require the use of both eyes are called _____.
    a. monocular cues
    b. diocular cues
    c. binocular cues
    d. dichromatic cues

Answers and Explanations to Multiple Choice Posttest

1. a. Sensation is the stimulation of a receptor cell, and perception is our interpretation of that stimulation.

2. c. Absolute threshold is a sensation detected 50% of the time.

3. d. Subliminal perception has not been shown to affect everyone in the same way.

4. b. The cornea is the protective coating on the outer layer of the eye.

5. c. The retina contains the receptor cells.

6. a. Rods and cones are receptors for light.

7. a. Rods are specialized for dim light.

8. b. Visual acuity refers to our ability to see fine details.

9. d. Glaucoma is the buildup of fluid pressure in the eye and results in damage to the optic nerve.

10. c. Mixing of pigments is called subtractive color mixing.

11. a. Both trichromatic and opponent-process theories are probably correct.

12. b. Pitch is the same as tone.

13. c. Hertz refers to the frequency of the sound wave.

14. d. The cochlea in the inner ear is curled up like a snail.

15. b. Flavor is a combination of taste and smell.

16. a. The skin is the largest sense organ and contains the most receptors.

17. b. Optical illusions are the result of distortions in perception.

18. d. Perceptual constancy enables us to see distant objects as the same size as when viewed close by.

19. d. Our cognitive style determines how we deal with our environment.

20. c. Binocular cues require both eyes.

Key Vocabulary Terms

Cut-out each term and use as study cards.
Definition is on the backside of each term.

Sensation	Pupil
Perception	Iris
Absolute threshold	Lens
Adaptation	Retina
Difference threshold	Fovea
Weber's Law	Receptor cell
Cornea	Rods

Small opening in the iris through which light enters the eye.	Experience of sensory stimulation.
Colored part of the eye.	Process of creating meaningful patterns from raw sensory information.
Transparent part of the eye inside the pupil that focuses light onto the retina.	The least amount of energy that can be detected as a stimulation 50 percent of the time.
Lining of the eye containing receptor cells that are sensitive to light.	Adjustment of the senses to stimulation.
Area of the retina that is the center of the visual field.	The smallest change in stimulation that can be detected 50 percent of the time.
Specialized cell that responds to a particular type of energy.	The principle that the just noticeable difference for any given sense is a constant proportion of the stimulation being judged.
Receptor cells in the retina responsible for night vision and perception of brightness.	The transparent protective coating over the front part of the eye.

Cones	Optic chiasm
Visual acuity	Hue
Dark adaptation	Saturation
Light adaptation	Brightness
Afterimage	Additive color mixing
Optic nerve	Subtractive color mixing
Blind spot	Trichromatic theory

Point near the base of the brain where some fibers in the optic nerve from each eye cross to the other side of the brain.	Receptor cells in the retina responsible for color vision.
The aspect of color that corresponds to names such as red, green, and blue.	The ability to distinguish fine details.
The vividness or richness of a hue.	Increased sensitivity of rods and cones in darkness.
The nearness of a color to white as opposed to black.	Decreased sensitivity of rods and cones in bright light.
The process of mixing lights of different wavelengths to create new hues.	Sense experience that occurs after a visual stimulus has been removed.
The process of mixing pigments, each of which absorbs some wavelengths of light and reflects others.	The bundle of axons of ganglion cells that carries neural messages from each eye to the brain.
Theory of color vision that holds that all color perception derives from three different color receptors in the retina (usually red, green, and blue receptors).	Place on the retina where the axons of all the ganglion cells leave the eye and where there are no receptors.

Colorblindness	Pitch
Trichromats	Amplitude
Monochromats	Decibel
Dichromats	Hammer, anvil, stirrup
Opponent-process theory	Oval window
Frequency	Round window
Hertz (Hz)	Cochlea

Auditory experience corresponding primarily to frequency of sound vibrations, resulting in a higher or lower tone.	Partial or total inability to perceive hues.
The magnitude of a wave; in sound, the primary determinant of loudness.	People who have normal color vision.
Unit of measurement for the loudness of sounds.	People who are totally colorblind.
The three small bones in the middle ear that relay vibrations of the eardrum to the inner ear.	People who are blind to either red-green or yellow-blue.
Membrane across the opening between the middle ear and inner ear that conducts vibrations to the cochlea.	Theory of color vision that holds that three sets of color receptors (yellow-blue, red-green, black-white) respond in an either/or fashion to determine the color you experience.
Membrane between the middle ear and inner ear that equalizes pressure in the inner ear.	The number of cycles per second in a wave; in sound, the primary determinant of pitch.
Part of the inner ear containing fluid that vibrates which in turn causes the basilar membrane to vibrate.	Cycles per second; unit of measurement for the frequency of waves.

Basilar membrane	Kinesthetic senses
Organ of Corti	Stretch receptors
Auditory nerve	Golgi tendon organs
Place theory	Vestibular sense
Frequency theory	Semicircular canals
Olfactory epithelium	Vestibular sacs
Pheromone	Gate control theory

Senses of forces and movement of muscles.	Vibrating membrane in the cochlea of the inner ear; it contains sense receptors for sound.
Receptors that sense muscle stretch and contraction.	Structure on the surface of the basilar membrane that contains the receptors cells for hearing.
Receptors that sense movement of the tendons, which connect muscle to bone.	The bundle of neurons that carries signals from each ear to the brain.
Senses of equilibrium and body position in space.	Theory that pitch is determined by the location of greatest vibration of the basilar membrane.
Structures in the inner ear particularly sensitive to body rotation.	Theory that pitch is determined by the frequency with which hair cells in the cochlea fire.
Sacs in the inner ear that are responsible for sensing gravitation and forward, backward, and vertical movement.	Nasal membranes containing receptor cells sensitive to odors.
Theory that a "neurological gate" in the spinal cord controls the transmission of pain messages to the brain.	Chemical that communicates information to other organisms through smell.

Figure	Monocular cues
Ground	Binocular cues
Perceptual constancy	Superposition
Size constancy	Linear perspective
Shape constancy	Motion parallax
Brightness constancy	Stereoscopic vision
Color constancy	Retinal disparity

Visual cues requiring the use of one eye.	Object perceived to stand apart from the background.
Visual cues requiring the use of both eyes.	Background against which the figure appears.
Monocular distance cue in which one object, by partly blocking a second object, is perceived as being closer.	Tendency to perceive objects as stable and unchanging despite changes in sensory stimulation.
Monocular cue to distance and depth based on the fact that two parallel lines seem to come together at the horizon.	Perception of an object as the same size regardless of the distance from which it is viewed.
Monocular distance cue in which objects closer than the point of visual focus seem to move in the direction opposite to viewer's moving head, and objects beyond the focus point seem to move in same direction.	Tendency to see an object as the same shape no matter what angle it is viewed from.
Combination of two retinal images to give a three-dimensional perceptual experience.	Perception of brightness as the same, even though the amount of light reaching the retina changes.
Binocular distance cue based on the difference between the images cast on the two retinas when both eyes are focused on the same object.	Inclination to perceive familiar objects as retaining their color despite changes in sensory information.

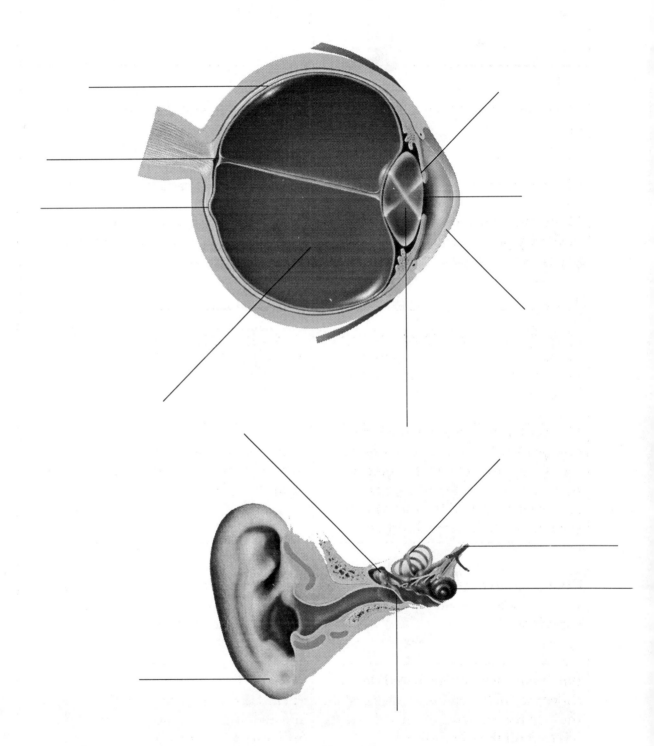

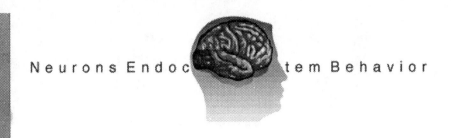
Neurons Endoc tem Behavior

Overview

• •

Natural Variations in Consciousness
Daydreaming and Fantasy
Sleep and Dreaming

Artificial Alternations in Consciousness
Meditation
Hypnosis

Drug-Altered Consciousness
Substance Use, Abuse, and Dependence
Depressants
Stimulants
Hallucinogens and Marijuana

States Of Consciousness

Class and Text Notes

This outline provides a way to organize your notes from both the text and the lecture. It will also serve as review sheets for the exam.

Natural Variations in Consciousness

Daydreaming and Fantasy

Sleep and Dreaming

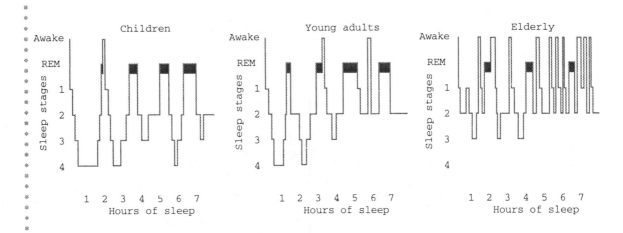

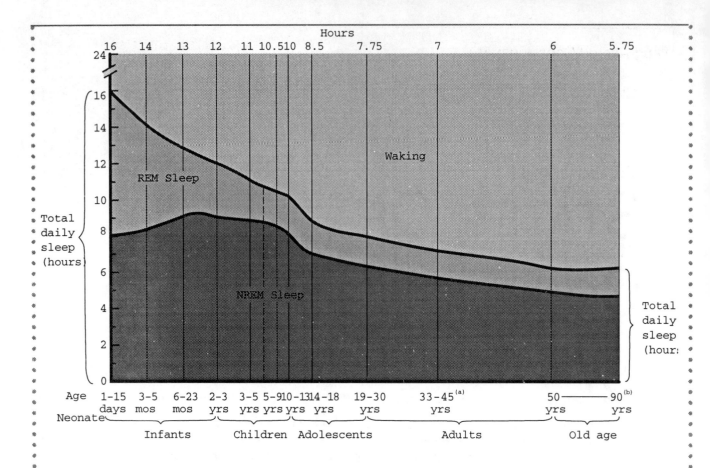

Artificial Alternations in Consciousness

Meditation

Hypnosis

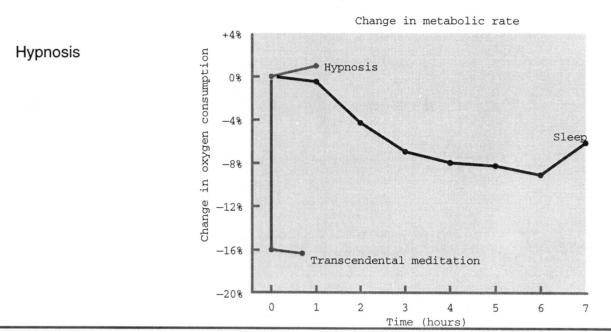

Change in metabolic rate

Drug-Altered Consciousness

Substance Use

Substance Abuse

Substance Dependence

Depressants

Stimulants

Hallucinogens and Marijuana

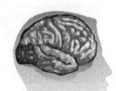

Multiple Choice Pretest

This pretest will help you identify the topics in the chapter that are most difficult for you. By focusing your study time in those areas, you will see the greatest improvement.

1. Which of the following is NOT an altered state of consciousness?
   a. meditation
   b. intoxication
   c. daydreaming
   d. concentration

2. Freud believed that the driving force behind all human behavior is _____.
   a. self-actualization
   b. positive reinforcement
   c. unconscious sexual/aggressive instincts
   d. human consciousness

3. Cycles of biological functions that are about 24 hours are known as _____.
   a. circadian
   b. diurnal
   c. infradian
   d. daiurnal

4. Rotating shifts at work can cause _____.
   a. ulcers
   b. sleep difficulties
   c. one to eat more than usual
   d. hypervigilence

5. Protein synthesis _____ during sleep.
   a. stays the same
   b. stops
   c. increases
   d. decreases

6. If someone is sleeping and her eyes begin to move rapidly while still closed, we would assume that she is in the _____ stage of sleep.
   a. Stage 1
   b. Stage 2
   c. Stage 3
   d. REM

7. _____ sleep can be called paradoxical sleep.
   a. Stage 1
   b. Stage 2
   c. Stage 3
   d. REM

8. About _____ % of the time people report vivid dreams when they are awakened in REM sleep.
   a. 20%
   b. 40%
   c. 60%
   d. 80%

9. Sleep terrors are most often found in _____.
   a. children under age 4
   b. children ages 4 to 12
   c. adolescents age 12 to 18
   d. young adults ages 18 to 30

10. If you want to wake someone up, which of the following is likely to be successful?
    a. flashing a light
    b. playing an alarm
    c. saying the sleeper's name
    d. shake the bed

11. What percent of people get too little sleep?
    a. 20%
    b. 25%
    c. 50%
    d. 80%

12. _____ is a sleep disorder in which a person has trouble falling asleep or remaining asleep.
    a. Apnea
    b. Cataplexy
    c. Narcolepsy
    d. Insomnia

13. _____ is a sleep disorder in which a person falls asleep suddenly many times a day.
    a. Apnea
    b. Cataplexy
    c. Narcolepsy
    d. Insomnia

14. A sleep disorder characterized by breathing difficulty at night and feelings of exhaustion during the day is _____.
    a. apnea
    b. cataplexy
    c. narcolepsy
    d. insomnia

15. Which of the following physiological changes is most likely to occur during meditation?
    a. higher rate of metabolism
    b. increase in beta waves
    c. increase in alpha waves
    d. increase in sympathetic nervous system activity

16. Which of the following is NOT true of hypnosis?
    a. It is useful in helping smokers temporarily reduce their smoking.
    b. Recall of events under regressive hypnosis has been shown to be extremely accurate for courtroom testimony.
    c. It has been found to be more effective than morphine in alleviating certain kinds of pain
    d. It has been shown to help hemophiliacs reduce their bleeding during dental treatment.

17. One out of every _____ deaths in the United States each year is related to smoking.
    a. 2   c. 10
    b. 6   d. 20

18. _____ is demonstrated when higher doses of a drug are required.
    a. Tolerance
    b. Potentiation
    c. Dependence
    d. Withdrawal

19. All of the following are depressants EXCEPT _____.
    a. alcohol
    b. cocaine
    c. opiates
    d. barbiturates

20. A subject in an antidepressant research study has been taking pills for 3 months. He will not find out, nor will the doctors giving him the pills, whether or not he has received the real drug or a placebo until after the study is over. The type of study he is involved in is called a _____.
    a. single-blind study
    b. double-blind study
    c. case study
    d. placebo study

Answers and Explanations to Multiple Choice Pretest

1. d. Meditation, daydreaming and intoxication are all altered states of consciousness.
2. c. Freud believed in unconscious drives.
3. a. Circadian means about a day.
4. b. Rotating shifts at work can lead to difficulty in sleeping.
5. c. Protein synthesis increases during sleep.
6. d. REM stage of sleep means rapid eye movements.
7. d. REM sleep is also called paradoxical sleep because a person's brain is very active.
8. d. If someone is awakened during REM sleep, 80% of the time dreams are remembered.
9. b. Night terrors occur in children 4-12 years of age.
10. c. The best way to wake someone up is to say their name.
11. c. 33-50% of adults do not get enough sleep.
12. d. Insomnia is trouble getting to sleep or staying asleep.
13. c. Narcolepsy is a disorder in which someone can suddenly fall asleep many time a day.
14. a. Someone with apnea stops breathing many time during the night.
15. c. Alpha brain waves result when someone is meditating.
16. b. Recall of information can be distorted during hypnosis which is a problem in court testimony.
17. b. One out of 6 deaths in America are related to smoking.
18. a. Requiring higher and higher amounts of a drug is called tolerance.
19. b. Cocaine is a stimulant not a depressant.
20. b. In a double-blind research study neither the subject nor the experimenter know if the subject is part of the control group or the treatment group.

Learning Objectives

After you have read and studied this chapter, you should be able to complete the following statements. Your exam is written based on these learning objectives.

1. Explain daydreaming.

2. Describe the stages of sleep and dreaming.

3. Explain why REM sleep is also called paradoxical sleep.

4. Explain the theories of the nature and content of dreams.

5. Define the sleep disorders of insomnia, narcolepsy, and apnea.

6. Describe meditation and hypnosis.

7. Explain the difference between substance abuse and substance dependence.

8. Explain the effects of depressants, stimulants, and hallucinogens.

9. Identify two conditions that can determine the effects of drugs.

10. List two negative effects of each of the following drugs: alcohol, marijuana, amphetamines, barbiturates, the opiates, cocaine, and the hallucinogens.

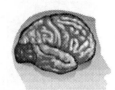

Short Essay Questions

Write out your answers to the following four essay questions to further your mastery of the topics.

1. Explain how circadium rhythms affect our functioning and also how disruptions in these rhythms can negatively affect people.

_____
_____
_____
_____
_____
_____
_____
_____
_____
_____
_____

2. Explain the possible uses of meditation.

_____
_____
_____
_____
_____
_____
_____
_____
_____
_____
_____

3. Describe narcolepsy, sleep apnea, and insomnia.

_____
_____
_____
_____
_____
_____
_____
_____
_____
_____

4. Describe the physical and psychological effects of stimulants and the problems associated with their use. _____

_____
_____
_____
_____
_____
_____
_____
_____
_____

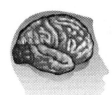

Language Support

Students identified the following words from the text as needing more explanation. This page can be cut-out, folded in half, and used as a bookmark for this chapter.

A-B-C-D

abstaining	not doing
achievement oriented	people who like to accomplish things
administration of the drug	give the drug
bizarre	very strange
business tycoon	rich business person
carnival	place where there are games and rides
colleagues	people they work with
commonsense	logical, makes sense
complicated	made more difficult
counterproductive	make the problem worse
curiosity	wanting to know about
definable	can be explained
depiction	picture
deprivation	not to have
deprived	do without
diminishes	make smaller
distinct	separate
dread	extreme fear
drowsiness	being very sleepy

E-F-G-H-I

effortless engagement	feeling connected without trying
enabled	helped
engaging in	doing
ensure	make sure
epidemic	problem that occurs with a lot of people
episodically	different points in time
euphoric	very happy
evidence	proof
fleeting	lasting only a short time
flow of subjective conscious experience	our personal experience of what is going on around us
harbingers	locations
heart palpitations	heart beating fast
hemophilia	a disease where a person bleeds too much
hiatus	vacation, time away from
hostile	angry
hypothesis	statement about what is going on
illogical	not reasonable
illusory	not real
immoral	wrong
implies	suggests
incapable	not able
insight	understanding
insomnia	not being able to sleep
intricate	fine and complicated

I-K-L-M-O-P-O

intriguing	very interesting
introspection	thinking about one's thoughts and feelings
irrelevant	not important
irritability	not patient with others
kaleidoscopic flow	many pictures blended together
landscapes	views outside of plants and hills
loosely connected	hard to find a relationship
massive	large
merely	only
midnight shift	work schedule that starts at midnight
mind is wandering	not thinking about what you should be
minor mishap	small problem
motives	reasons for
narrative	story
negligible	very small
nourished	feed
outbursts	sudden activity
overwhelming array	too many different types
paralyzed	cannot move muscles
phenomenon	occurrence
pinprick	being stuck and hurt with a pin
placebo	believed to have active ingredient but does not
precautions	being very careful
predisposition	more likely to
preoccupied	busy
primitive	very basic
proposing	stating, suggesting
pursued	someone chasing them
quick jolt	fast return

R

reminisce	remember
repetitious	something that repeats over and over again
resembling it	looking like it
rudimentary	basic
sequential	happening in order
spectacular	very impressive and important
spy thrillers	exciting movies about spy activity
stage-manage	boss at a play (drama)
strenuous	difficult
subtleties	small points

T-U-V-W

tantamount	the same things as
tapering off	decreasing in amount
tossing and turning	moving a lot while sleeping
"twilight" state	half asleep and half awake
unbeknownst	did not know
uncomplicated	not confused
unimpaired	working well
unpredictable	cannot be known in advance
verifiable	can be proven
victimized	hurt
wholehearted	complete
window of opportunity	a chance

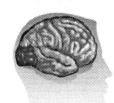

Multiple Choice Posttest

After studying the text and completing the Study Guide activities, answer these questions to determine if you need to review any areas before the course exam.

1. James developed the idea of the flow of conscious ideas and information resembling a
   a. tide.
   b. lake.
   c. stream.
   d. wind.

2. According to Singer, daydreams
   _____.
   a. are an important part of our ability to process information.
   b. are the result of unfulfilled sexual desires
   c. are the equivalent of a mental vacation from reality
   d. are a retreat from the real world and have no practical value

3. Our sleeping-waking cycle follows a
   _____ rhythm.
   a. ultradian
   b. monournal
   c. diurnal
   d. circadian

4. People may be able to adjust their biological clocks to prevent jet lag by taking small amount of the hormone _____.
   a. serotonin   c. dopamine
   b. epinephrin   d. melatonin

5. Which of the following is NOT seen in REM sleep?
   a. paralysis of body muscles
   b. periods of REM sleep get shorter as the night continues
   c. rapid eye movement
   d. arousal of brain activity

6. Who sleeps the longest?
   a. infants
   b. children
   c. adolescents
   d. elderly

7. Freud believed that sleep and dreams expressed ideas that were free from the _____.
   a. memories of worrisome daily events
   b. instinctive feelings of anger, jealousy, or ambition
   c. conscious controls and moral rules
   d. case study method

8. Research appears to be supporting the hypothesis that REM sleep _____.
   a. reflects the brain's efforts to stimulate itself
   b. is related to restoration and growth at the neurophysiological level
   c. dreams are generated by random outbursts of nerve activity
   d. dreams reflect the brain's effort to free itself of irrelevant and repetitious thoughts

9. Which of the following is NOT a suggestion to help overcome insomnia?
   a. establish regular sleeping habits
   b. have a strong alcoholic drink before bed
   c. change bedtime routine
   d. get out of bed and do someting until feeling sleepy

10. _____ is a sleep disorder in which a person has trouble falling asleep or remaining asleep.
    a. Apnea   c. Narcolepsy
    b. Cataplexy   d. Insomnia

11. _____ is a sleep disorder in which a person falls asleep suddenly many times a day.
    a. Apnea   c. Narcolepsy
    b. Cataplexy   d. Insomnia

12. A sleep disorder characterized by breathing difficulty at night and feelings of exhaustion during the day is _____.
    a. apnea   c. narcolepsy
    b. cataplexy   d. insomnia

13. In the double-blind procedure, some subjects receive a medication while the control group receives an inactive substance called _____.
    a. control treatment
    b. Hawthorne reactor
    c. a placebo
    d. dependent variable

14. Some people experience alcohol as a(n) _____ because it inhibits centers in the brain that are used in higher-level thinking and inhibition of impulsive behavior.
    a. stimulant
    b. depressant
    c. hallucinogenic
    d. antigen

15. Recent research in Denmark indicates that alcohol _____.
    a. kills brain cells
    b. causes brain cells to dedifferentiate
    c. disconnects brain cells from each other
    d. all of the above

16. Drugs such as heroin that dull the senses and induce feelings of euphoria and relaxation are _____.
    a. hallucinogens
    b. opiates
    c. barbiturates
    d. placebos

17. All of the following are withdrawal symptoms from heavy coffee use EXCEPT _____.
    a. depression
    b. insomnia
    c. lethargy
    d. headaches

18. Smoking increases _____ in the pleasure centers of the brain.
    a. endorphins
    b. acetylcholine
    c. dopamine
    d. norepinephrine

19. Mescaline, peyote, and psilocybin are all _____.
    a. stimulants   c. barbiturates
    b. opiates   d. hallucinogens

Answers and Explanations to Multiple Choice Posttest

1. c. James described the flow of consciousness like a stream

2. a. Singer believes daydreaming is important to process information.

3. d. Circadian rhythms include a daily sleep and awake cycle.

4. d. A small amount of melatonin may prevent jet lag.

5. b. Periods of REM get longer throughout the night, not shorter.

6. a. Infants require the most sleep.

7. c. Dreams were thought by Freud to be free from conscious controls and moral rules.

8. b. Research supports that REM sleep is involved with restoration.

9. b. Alcohol interferes with getting a good night's sleep.

10. d. Insomnia is trouble getting to sleep or staying asleep.

11. c. Narcolepsy is a disorder in which someone can suddenly fall asleep many time a day.

12. a. Someone with apnea stops breathing many time during the night.

13. c. A placebo is an inactive substance given to the control group.

14. a. Alcohol may be experienced as a stimulant because it decreases our inhibitions.

15. c. Alcohol may disconnect brain cells from each other.

16. b. Heroin is an opiate.

17. b. Caffeine withdrawal does not usually interfere with sleep because a person tends to be very sleepy.

18. c. Smoking increases dopamine in the pleasure centers.

19. d. Mescaline, peyote and psilocybin are all hallucinogens.

Consciousness	Apnea
Waking consciousness	Narcolepsy
Altered state of consciousness	Meditation
REM (paradoxical) sleep	Hypnosis
Non-REM (NREM) sleep	Psychoactive drugs
Dreams	Substance abuse
Insomnia	Substance dependence

Sleep disorder characterized by breathing difficulty during the night and feelings of exhaustion during the day.	Our awareness of various cognitive processes, such as sleeping, dreaming, concentrating, and making decisions.
Hereditary sleep disorder characterized by sudden nodding off during the day and sudden loss of muscle tone following moments of emotional excitement.	Mental state that includes the thoughts, feelings, and perceptions that occur when we are awake and reasonably alert.
Any of various methods of concentration, reflection, or focusing of thoughts undertaken to reduce the activity of the sympathetic nervous system.	Mental state that differs noticeably from normal waking consciousness.
Trancelike state in which the subject responds readily to suggestions.	Sleep stage characterized by rapid eye movement; it is during this stage that most vivid dreaming occurs.
Chemical substances that change moods and perceptions.	Non-rapid-eye-movement stages of sleep that alternate with REM stages during the sleep cycle.
A pattern of drug use that diminishes the user's ability to fulfill responsibilities at home, work or school, that results in repeated use of a drug in dangerous situations, legal problems.	Vivid visual and auditory experiences that occur primarily during REM periods of sleep.
A pattern of compulsive drug taking that often results in tolerance and-or withdrawal.	Sleep disorder characterized by difficulty in falling asleep or remaining asleep throughout the night.

Tolerance	Opiates
Withdrawal symptoms	Stimulants
Double-blind procedure	Amphetamines
Placebo	Cocaine
Depressants	Hallucinogens
Alcohol	LSD
Barbiturates	Marijuana

Drugs, such as opium and heroin, derived from the opium poppy, that dull the senses and induce feelings of euphoria, and relaxation. Synthetic drugs resembling opium derivatives are also considered opiates.	Phenomenon whereby higher doses of a drug are required to produce its original effects or to prevent withdrawal symptoms.
Drugs, including amphetamines, and cocaine, that stimulate the sympathetic nervous system and produce feelings of optimism and boundless energy.	Unpleasant physical or psychological effects that follow the discontinuance of a dependence-producing substance.
Stimulant drugs that initially produce "rushes" of euphoria often followed by sudden "crashes" and, sometimes, severe depression.	Experiment in which neither the subject nor the researcher know which subjects are receiving the treatment.
Drug derived from the cocoa plant that, while producing a sense of euphoria by stimulating the sympathetic nervous system, also produces anxiety, depression, and addictive cravings.	Chemically inactive substance used for comparison with active drugs in experiments on the effects of drugs.
Any of a number of drugs, such as LSD and mescaline, that distort visual and auditory perception.	Chemicals that slow down behavior or cognitive processes.
Hallucinogen or "psychedelic" drug that produces hallucinations and delusions similar to those occurring in a psychotic state.	Depressant that is the intoxicating ingredient in whiskey, beer, wine, and other fermented or distilled liquors.
Plant containing a mild hallucinogen that produces a "high" often characterized by feelings of euphoria, a sense of well-being, and swings in mood from gaiety to relaxation.	Potentially deadly depressants, first used for their sedative and anticonvulsant effects, now used only to treat such conditions as epilepsy and arthritis.

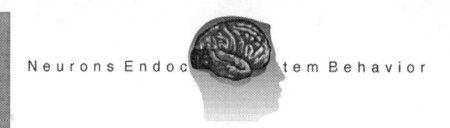
Neurons Endoc tem Behavior

Overview

● ●

Classical Conditioning
Pavlov's Conditioning Experiments
Elements of Classical Conditioning
Classical Conditioning In Humans
Classical Conditioning Is Selective

Operant Conditioning
Thorndike's Conditioning Experiments
Elements of Operant Conditioning
Type Of Reinforcement
Punishment
Operant Conditioning Is Selective
Superstitious Behavior

Comparing Classical And Operant Conditioning
Response Acquisition in Classical and
    Operant Conditioning
Extinction and Spontaneous Recovery
    in Classical Conditioning
Extinction and Spontaneous Recovery
    in Operant Conditioning
Generalization and Discrimination in
    Classical Conditioning
Generalization and Discrimination in
    Operant Conditioning

New Learning Based on Original Learning
Higher-Order Conditioning in
    Classical Conditioning
Secondary Reinforcers in Operant
    Conditioning

Contingencies Are Important
Contingencies in Classical
    Conditioning
Contingencies in Operant
    Conditioning

A Review of Classical Conditioning and Operant Conditioning

Cognitive Learning
Cognitive Maps and Latent Learning
Insight and Learning Sets

Learning by Observing

Cognitive Learning in Nonhumans

108   CHAPTER 5

LEARNING

5

Class and Text Notes

This outline provides a way to organize your notes from both the text and the lecture. It will also serve as review sheets for the exam.

Classical Conditioning

    Pavlov's Conditioning Experiments

    Elements of Classical Conditioning

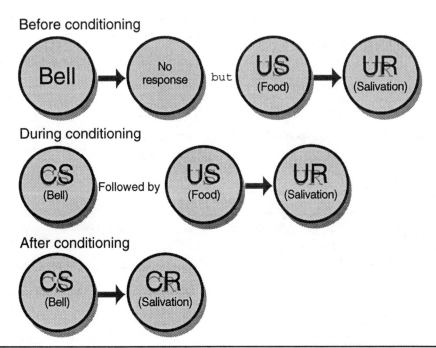

Before conditioning

Bell → No response   but   US (Food) → UR (Salivation)

During conditioning

CS (Bell)   Followed by   US (Food) → UR (Salivation)

After conditioning

CS (Bell) → CR (Salivation)

Classical Conditioning In Humans

Classical Conditioning Is Selective

Operant Conditioning

Thorndike's Conditioning Experiments

Elements of Operant Conditioning

Type Of Reinforcement

Punishment

Operant Conditioning Is Selective

Superstitious Behavior

Comparing Classical And Operant Conditioning

Response Acquisition in Classical and Operant Conditioning

Extinction and Spontaneous Recovery in Classical Conditioning

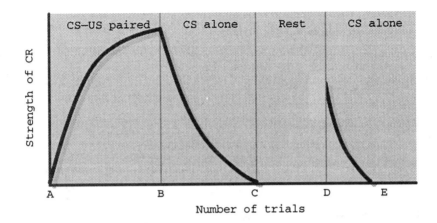

Extinction and Spontaneous Recovery in Operant Conditioning

Generalization and Discrimination in Classical Conditioning

Generalization and Discrimination in Operant Conditioning

New Learning Based on Original Learning

Higher-Order Conditioning in Classical Conditioning

Secondary Reinforcers in Operant Conditioning

Contingencies Are Important

Contingencies in Classical Conditioning

Contingencies in Operant Conditioning

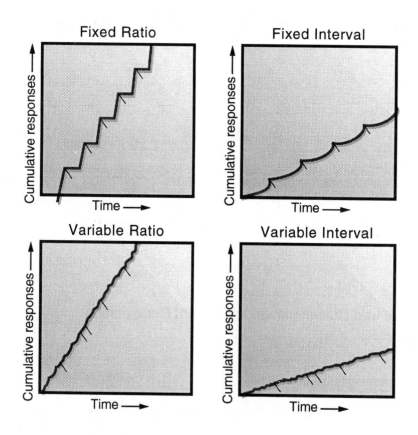

A Review of Classical Conditioning and Operant Conditioning

Cognitive Learning

Cognitive Maps and Latent Learning

Insight and Learning Sets

Learning by Observing

Cognitive Learning in Nonhumans

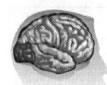

Multiple Choice Pretest

This pretest will help you identify the topics in the chapter that are most difficult for you. By focusing your study time in those areas, you will see the greatest improvement.

1. The process of learning is defined as experience resulting in _____.
   a. amplification of sensory stimuli
   b. delayed genetic behavioral contributions
   c. relatively permanent behavior change
   d. acquisition of motivation

2. Operant conditioning is another term for _____.
   a. instrumental conditioning
   b. cognitive restructuring
   c. observational learning
   d. classical conditioning

3. By pairing the ringing of the bell with the presentation of meat, Pavlov trained dogs to salivate to the sound of a bell even when no meat was presented. In this experiment, the presentation of the meat was the _____.
   a. unconditioned stimulus
   b. conditioned stimulus
   c. unconditioned response
   d. conditioned response

4. You have a cat that runs to the sound of the cat food cabinet opening. The sound of the cabinet is the _____.
   a. unconditioned stimulus
   b. conditioned stimulus
   c. unconditioned response
   d. conditioned response

5. In the experiment with Little Albert, the unconditioned stimulus was _____.
   a. the experimenter
   b. the rat
   c. the loud noise
   d. the laboratory

6. Classical conditioning is relate to _____ therapy.
   a. response
   b. psychoanalytic
   c. conditioned
   d. desensitization

7. Which of the following is NOT an example of operantly learned behavior?
   a. eye blinking after a flash of light is presented
   b. a child studying in order to get a teacher's approval
   c. a rat pressing a bar after receiving food for this behavior
   d. a rat pressing a bar to avoid a shock for this behavior

8. Operant conditioning is based on the principle that behaviors occur more often when they are _____
   a. punished   c. reinforced
   b. modeled   d. ignored

9. Any stimulus that follows a behavior and increases the likelihood that the behavior will be repeated is called a _____.
   a. cue
   b. situational stimulus
   c. reinforcer
   d. higher-order conditioner

10. Any stimulus that follows a behavior and decreases the likelihood that the behavior will be repeated is called a _____.
    a. cue
    b. situational stimulus
    c. reinforcer
    d. punisher

11. A reinforcer that adds something rewarding is a _____.
    a. secondary reinforcer c. triary reinforcer
    b. positive reinforcer   d. negative reinforcer

12. A reinforcer that increases the likelihood of the behavior because a person wants to avoid the reinforcer is called _____ reinforcement.
    a. secondary   c. triary
    b. positive   d. negative

13. Each of the following is true of punishment EXCEPT _____.
    a. it can make people more aggressive and hostile
    b. it teaches more desirable behavior
    c. it can disrupt the learning process
    d. the negative behavior may be only suppressed and not changed

14. A problem that may result from avoidance training is _____.
    a. a person may continue to avoid something which no longer needs to be avoided
    b. its effects tend to last for only a short time
    c. that it may produce latent learning
    d. it tends to take effect when it is too late to make a difference in avoiding the problem situation

15. When an extinguished behavior suddenly reappears on its own, with no retraining, the process is called _____.
    a. discrimination
    b. generalization
    c. extinction
    d. spontaneous recovery

16. A person originally feared only spiders but now also fears other types of insects. These new fears are probably the result of
    _____.
    a. stimulus generalization
    b. response generalization
    c. obedience
    d. pain thresholds

17. Food and water are _____ .
    a. delayed reinforcer
    b. primary reinforcer
    c. secondary reinforcer
    d. direct reinforcer

18. If you work a job where you get paid a salary every 2 weeks, you are being reinforced on a _____ schedule.
    a. fixed-ratio
    b. fixed-interval
    c. variable-ratio
    d. variable-interval

19. Unannounced quizzes are _____ schedules of reinforcement
    a. fixed-ratio   c. variable
    b. fixed-interval   d. variable-interval

Answers and Explanations to Multiple Choice Pretest

1. c. Learning is defined as the relatively permanent behavioral change that results from experience.

2. a. Operant conditioning is the same thing as instrument conditioning.

3. a. The meat is the unconditional stimulus.

4. b. The cat **learned** to respond to the sound of the cabinet, therefore the sound is a conditioned stimulus.

5. c. Little Albert reacted to the unconditioned (unlearned) stimulus of the loud noise.

6. d. Desensitization is classical conditioning because a person learns to associate a new response to a stimulus.

7. a. Eye blinking is an unconditioned stimulus in classical conditioning NOT operant conditioning.

8. c. Reinforcement increases the likelihood of the behavior.

9. c. Once again, reinforcement increases the likelihood of the behavior.

10. d. Punishment decreases the likelihood of the behavior.

11. b. Positive reinforcement adds a reward.

12. d. Negative reinforcement increases behavior to avoid negative consequence.

13. b. Punishment does NOT teach any new behavior.

14. a. Avoidance training is a problem if the person keeps avoiding something when he no longer needs to.

15. d. Spontaneous recovery is the return of extinguished behavior without additional training.

16. a. The new fears are the result of stimulus generalization.

17. b. Primary reinforcement is food and water.

18. b. You are on a fixed-interval schedule when you are paid a salary every 2 weeks.

19. d. Unannounced quizzes are a variable-interval schedule.

Learning Objectives

After you have read and studied this chapter, you should be able to complete the following statements. Your exam is written based on these learning objectives.

1. Describe how classical conditioning was discovered. Define: unconditioned stimulus, unconditioned response, conditioned stimulus, and conditioned response.

2. Describe the experiment with little Albert. Describe desensitization therapy.

3. List the factors necessary for the success of learning in classical conditioning.

4. Explain these processes: extinction, spontaneous recovery, inhibition, stimulus generalization, discrimination, and higher-order conditioning.

5. Distinguish between classical and operant conditioning.

6. Explain the principle of reinforcement. Define primary reinforcer and secondary reinforcer and give examples of each.

7. Explain the effects of delay of reinforcement.

8. Identify four schedules of reinforcement and the pattern of response associated with each.

9. Define positive reinforcement.

10. Explain how to use punishment successfully.

11. Define negative reinforcement. Explain the process of avoidance training.

12. Distinguish between cognitive learning and traditional theories of conditioning. Explain contingency theory.

13. Discuss social learning theory and its implications for human learning.

14. Define learning set and describe the phenomenon of insight learning.

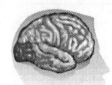

Short Essay Questions

Write out your answers to the following four essay questions to further your mastery of the topics.

1. Give two examples of classical conditioning in your own life, naming the US, UR, CS, and CR.

_____

_____

_____

_____

_____

_____

_____

_____

_____

_____

_____

2. Describe generalization and discrimination that occur in classical conditioning.

_____

_____

_____

_____

_____

_____

_____

_____

3. Explain the importance of contingencies in classical conditioning.

_____

_____

_____

_____

_____

_____

_____

_____

_____

_____

_____

4. Explain Bandura's study on aggression. ____

_____

_____

_____

_____

_____

_____

_____

_____

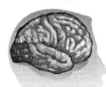

Language Support

Students identified the following words from the text as needing more explanation. This page can be cut-out, folded in half, and used as a bookmark for this chapter.

A
advocates — people in favor of
anecdotal — from life experiences but not research

C
charted — to draw the information onto a graph
conducive to — promotes, helpful to
consequences — that which comes after something
construct — make
cruel — very mean

D
deprived — not given
diminishing — decreasing
discount — think of as less important
drooled — mouth watered

E
electrical outlets — wall socket where electrical cords are plugged
elicited — caused
ensure — make sure
entity — thing
exclaimed — said

F
food hopper — container for food
forbidden — can not do

H
handguns — small gun, not a long rifle
high-wire performer — someone that does trick walking on a wire high in the air

I
inflicting — causing to happen
ingrained — part of us
invariably — always
irrelevant — not important
item — thing

L
linked — connected, associated
littering — throwing trash on the ground

M
metronome — a device to keep time when playing a musical instrument
misdeed — mistake
mispronounce — not say work correctly

N
nausea — feeling sick to the stomach
not inevitable — will not definitely happen
notable exception — important area it does not apply
novel — new

O

overt	can be seen

P

panacea	cure for everything
pedestal	raised stand
persist	continue to happen
personal hygiene	people cleaning their bodies, hair and clothing
placidly	calmly

Q

quackery	false medical treatment

R

rapid	fast
recklessly	not carefully
remarkable	very important
rubber mallet	hammer made out of rubber

S

scolds	punish verbally
spontaneous	happens suddenly
squash	game where a ball is hit against a wall with a paddle
startle	to be suddenly surprised
startling	scary
steel mesh	steel (metal) net
successive day	one day after the other
suppress	decrease
surroundings	environment
surveyed	studied through the use of a questionnaire
sustaining	keeping

T

tedious	boring
terminating	stopping

U

uncooperative	would not work together
unsafe sexual behavior	sexual activities that can result in sexually transmitted diseases

V

vicarious	learning by just watching others

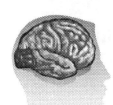

Multiple Choice Posttest

After studying the text and completing the Study Guide activities, answer these questions to determine if you need to review any areas before the course exam.

1. Conditioning can result in _____, which are irrational fears of particular things, activities, or situations.
   a. response generalization
   b. generalized anxieties
   c. phobias
   d. secondary reinforcement

2. In the experiment with Little Albert, the conditioned response was _____.
   a. fear of the experimenter
   b. fear of the laboratory
   c. fear of the rat
   d. fear of the loud noise

3. Any stimulus that follows a behavior and increases the likelihood that the behavior will be repeated is called a _____.
   a. cue
   b. situational stimulus
   c. reinforcer
   d. higher-order conditioner

4. Any stimulus that follows a behavior and decreases the likelihood that the behavior will be repeated is called a _____.
   a. cue
   b. situational stimulus
   c. reinforcer
   d. punisher

5. A reinforcer that adds something rewarding is a _____.
   a. secondary reinforcer   c. triary reinforcer
   b. positive reinforcer   d. negative reinforcer

6. A reinforcer that increases the likelihood of the behavior because a person wants to avoid the reinforcer is called _____ reinforcement.
   a. secondary   c. triary
   b. positive   d. negative

7. _____ therapy for treating anxiety involves the pairing of relaxation training with systematic exposure to the fearful thing.

   a. operant conditioning
   b. shaping
   c. aversive conditioning
   d. desensitization

8. Taking vitamins to prevent illnesses is called _____ training.
   a. aversion
   b. avoidance
   c. shaping
   d. classical conditioning

9. Reacting to a stimulus that is similar to one that you have already learned to react to is called _____.
   a. response generalization
   b. modeling
   c. higher-order conditioning
   d. stimulus generalization

10. A dolphin learns to swim toward a blue platform but not toward another platform of a different color. This shows the concept of _____.
    a. discrimination
    b. modeling
    c. higher-order conditioning
    d. stimulus generalization

11. Which of the following is a primary reinforcer? _____.
    a. ticket to a show
    b. a buzzer
    c. money
    d. candy

12. In partial reinforcement, the plan for when to reinforce correct behaviors is called a _____.
    a. response-to-reinforcement guide
    b. token economy
    c. schedule of reinforcement
    d. reinforcement map

13. Gambling behavior is being reinforced on a
_____ schedule.
    a. ratio-interval
    b. fixed-interval
    c. variable-ratio
    d. variable-interval

14. Learning that depends on mental processes that
are not able to be observed directly is called
_____ learning.
    a. cognitive
    b. neurophysiological learning
    c. secondary learning
    d. primary

15. The type of learning that involves elements
suddenly coming together so that the solution to
a problem is clear is called _____.
    a. latent learning
    b. insight
    c. cognitive mapping
    d. vicarious learning

16. The mental picture of an area, such as the floor
plan of a building is called _____.
    a. a perceptual illusion
    b. a mental set
    c. subliminal perception
    d. a cognitive map

17. Becoming increasingly more effective in solving
problems as one experiences solving problems is
called _____..
    a. a learning set
    b. a response cue
    c. latent learning
    d. a response set

18. The ability to learn by observing a model or
receiving instructions, without reinforcement, is
called _____ theory.
    a. cognitive learning
    b. contingency
    c. social learning
    d. classical conditioning

19. An operant conditioning technique in which a
learner gains control over some biological
response is _____.
    a. contingency training
    b. preparedness
    c. social learning
    d. biofeedback

Answers and Explanations to Multiple Choice Posttest

1. c. Conditioning can result in phobias.
2. c. Conditioned (learned) to fear the rat because it was paired with a loud noise.
3. c. Reinforcement increases behavior.
4. d. Punishment decreases the behavior.
5. b. Positive reinforcement adds a reward.
6. d. Negative reinforcement increases behavior to avoid a negative.
7. d. Desensitization involves progressive relaxation combined with systematic exposure to the feared thing.
8. b. We take vitamins to avoid illness, therefore this is called avoidance training.
9. d. Reacting to another stimulus is called stimulus generalization.
10. a. Discrimination occurs when an animal is able to tell the difference between stimuli and only respond to one.
11. d. Candy is a primary reinforcer.
12. c. Schedule of reinforcement is when reinforcement is partial and done according to specific plans.
13. c. Gambling is variable-ratio.
14. a. Cognitive learning is not directly seen through behavior.
15. b. Insight is a sudden solution to a problem.
16. d. Mental picture is a cognitive map.
17. a. A learning set enables us to learn by doing.
18. c. Social learning theory explains learning from a role model.
19. d. Biofeedback is gaining control of a biological response.

Learning	Conditioned response
Conditioning	Desensitization therapy
Classical or Pavlovian conditioning	Taste aversion
Operant or instrumental conditioning	Operant behavior
Unconditioned stimulus (US)	Reinforcer
Unconditioned response (UR)	Punisher
Conditioned stimulus	Law of effect

After conditioning, the response an organism produces when only a conditioned stimulus is presented.	The process by which experience or practice results in a relatively permanent change in behavior or potential behavior.
Conditioning technique designed to gradually reduce anxiety about a particular object or situation.	The acquisition of specific patterns of behavior in the presence of well-defined stimuli.
Conditioned avoidance of poisonous food.	Type of learning in which a response naturally elicited by one stimulus comes to be elicited by a different, neutral stimulus.
Behavior designed to operate on the environment in a way that will gain something desired or avoid something unpleasant.	Type of learning in which behaviors are emitted (in the presence of specific stimuli) to earn rewards to avoid punishments.
A stimulus that follows a behavior and increases the likelihood that the behavior will be repeated.	Stimulus that invariably causes an organism to respond in a specific way.
A stimulus that follows a behavior and decreases the likelihood that the behavior will be repeated.	Response that takes place in an organism whenever an unconditioned stimulus occurs.
Thorndike's theory that behavior consistently rewarded will be "stamped in " as learned behavior.	Originally neutral stimulus that is paired with an unconditioned stimulus and eventually produces the desired response in an organism when presented alone.

Positive reinforcer	Extinction
Negative reinforcer	Spontaneous recovery
Avoidance training	Stimulus generalization
Response acquisition	Stimulus discrimination
Intermittent pairing	Response generalization
Skinner box	Primary reinforcer
Shaping	Secondary reinforcer

Decrease in the strength or frequency of a learned response due to failure to continue pairing the US and CS (classical conditioning) or the withholding of reinforcement (operant conditioning).	Any event whose presence increases the likelihood that ongoing behavior will recur.
The reappearance of an extinguished response after the passage of time.	Any event whose reduction or termination increases the likelihood that ongoing behavior will recur.
Transfer of a learned response to different but similar stimuli	Learning a desirable behavior to prevent an unpleasant condition such as punishment from occurring.
Learning to respond to only one stimulus and to inhibit the response to all other stimuli.	"Building phase" of the conditioning during which the likelihood or strength of the desired response increases.
Giving a response that is somewhat different from the response originally learned to that stimulus.	Pairing the conditioned stimulus and the unconditioned stimulus on only a portion of the learning trials.
Reinforcer that is rewarding in itself, such as food, water, and sex.	Box that is often used in operant conditioning of animals. It limits the available responses and thus increases the likelihood that the desired response will occur.
Reinforcer whose value is learned through association with other primary or secondary reinforcers.	Reinforcing successive approximations of a desired behavior.

Contingency	Cognitive learning
Blocking	Latent learning
Schedule of reinforcement	Cognitive map
Fixed-interval schedule	Learning set
Variable-interval schedule	Social learning theory
Fixed-ratio schedule	Observational learning
Variable-ratio schedule	Vicarious reinforcement/punishment

Learning that depends on mental processes that are not directly observable.	A reliable "if-then" relationship between two events such as a CS and US.
Learning that is not immediately reflected in a behavior change.	Prior conditioning prevents conditioning to a second stimulus even when the two stimuli are presented simultaneously.
A learned mental image of a spatial environment that may be called on to solve problems when stimuli in the environment change.	In partial reinforcement, the rule for determining when and how often reinforcers will be delivered.
Ability to become increasingly more effective in solving problems as more problems are solved.	Reinforcement schedule that calls for reinforcement of a correct response after a fixed length of time.
View of learning that emphasizes the ability to learn by observing a model or receiving instructions, without firsthand experience by the learner.	Reinforcement schedule in which a correct response is reinforced after varying lengths of time after the last reinforcement.
Learning by observing other people's behavior.	Reinforcement schedule in which the correct response is reinforced after a fixed number of correct responses.
Performance of behaviors learned through observation that is modified by watching others who are reinforced or punished for their behavior.	Reinforcement schedule in which a varying number of correct responses must occur before reinforcement is presented.

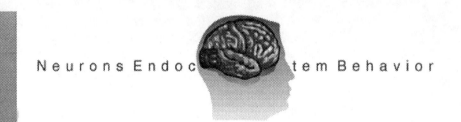

Neurons Endoc tem Behavior

Overview

• •

The Sensory Registers
Visual and Auditory Registers
Initial Processing

Short-Term Memory
Capacity of STM
Retention and Retrieval in STM
Rote Rehearsal
Elaborative Rehearsal

Long-Term Memory
Coding in LTM
Implicit Memory
Storage and Retrieval in LTM
Autobiographical Memory

Special Topics in Memory
Flashbulb Memories
Improving Your Memory

Biological Bases of Memory

MEMORY

6

Class and Text Notes

This outline provides a way to organize your notes from both the text and the lecture. It will also serve as review sheets for the exam.

The Sensory Registers

Visual and Auditory Registers

Initial Processing

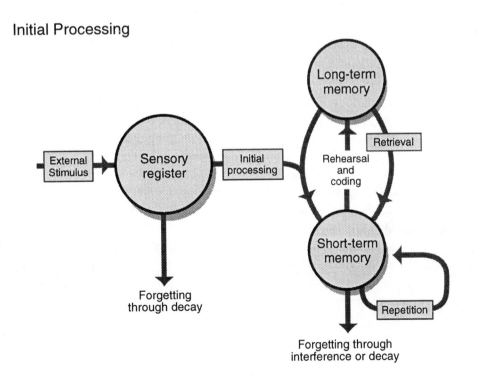

Short-Term Memory

Capacity of STM

Retention and Retrieval in STM

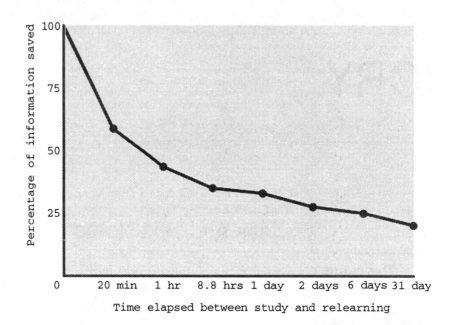

Rote Rehearsal

Elaborative Rehearsal

Long-Term Memory

Coding in LTM

Implicit Memory

Storage and Retrieval in LTM

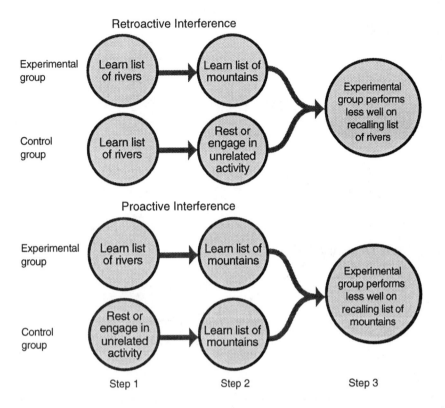

Retroactive Interference

Experimental group: Learn list of rivers → Learn list of mountains → Experimental group performs less well on recalling list of rivers

Control group: Learn list of rivers → Rest or engage in unrelated activity →

Proactive Interference

Experimental group: Learn list of rivers → Learn list of mountains → Experimental group performs less well on recalling list of mountains

Control group: Rest or engage in unrelated activity → Learn list of mountains →

Step 1   Step 2   Step 3

Autobiographical Memory

SUMMARY TABLE

Types of Memory

Type of Memory	Definition	Example
Semantic memory	Portion of long-term memory that stores general facts and information	Recalling the capital of Ohio
Episodic memory	Portion of long-term memory that stores specific information that has personal meaning	Recalling where you went on your first date
Implicit memory	Memory for information that either was not intentionally committed to memory or that is retrieved unintentionally from memory	Suddenly thinking of a friend's name without knowing why

Special Topics in Memory

Flashbulb Memories

Improving Your Memory

Biological Bases of Memory

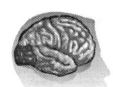

Multiple Choice Pretest

This pretest will help you identify the topics in the chapter that are most difficult for you. By focusing your study time in those areas, you will see the greatest improvement.

1. Ebbinghaus found that _____.
   a. the rate of forgetting was slow during the first few hours, increased during the period of 6 to 12 hours after learning, then decreased again after 12 hours
   b. the rate of forgetting increased after the first few hours
   c. most forgetting occurred in the first few hours, then leveled off
   d. forgetting occurred at a fairly even pace

2. A process by which a person continues to study material even after it has been learned is called _____.
   a. eidetic learning
   b. mnemonic learning
   c. semantic learning
   d. overlearning

3. Sensory registers _____.
   a. receive sensory information from the external world
   b. retain past information
   c. are measures of retention
   d. control our attention span

4. The process of selective looking, listening, smelling, and feeling is called _____.
   a. recall
   b. recognition
   c. attention
   d. social

5. Working memory and _____ mean the same thing.
   a. eidetic memory
   b. flashbulb memory
   c. long-term memory
   d. short-term memory

6. The most accurate description of short-term memory's capacity is probably to say that it can hold _____.
   a. as much information as can be heard on 1 to 4 seconds

   b. as much information as can be rehearsed in 1.5 to 2 seconds
   c. between 5 and 10 bits of information
   d. as much information as can be read in 3 to 5 seconds

7. _____ results in more material being stored in short-term memory because the information is grouped together.
   a. Categorizing
   b. Rehearsal
   c. Cueing
   d. Chunking

8. Material stored in short-term memory remains there for about _____.
   a. .25 seconds
   b. 4 microseconds
   c. one second
   d. 15 -20 seconds

9. Repeating information over and over again to retain it in short-term memory is called

   _____.
   a. deep processing
   b. rote rehearsal
   c. overlearning
   d. elaborative rehearsal

10. Connecting new information to material which is already known is called

    _____.
    a. overlearning
    b. rote rehearsal
    c. elaborative learning
    d. chunking

11. The type of memory that is usually permanent and stores what we know is called

    _____.
    a. eidetic memory
    b. working memory
    c. primary memory
    d. long-term memory

12. The definition of a key term from your psychology text is most likely stored in _____ memory.
    a. elaborative
    b. episodic
    c. semantic
    d. procedural

13. The portion of long-term memory that stores specific information that has personal meaning is called _____ memory
    a. semantic
    b. eidetic
    c. rehearsal
    d. episodic

14. Research on implicit and explicit memory indicates that _____.
    a. people with amnesia are more likely to lose implicit than explicit memory
    b. anesthesia blocks out implicit, but not explicit, memories
    c. the setting in which you learned information can serve as a retrieval cue to help you later recall that material
    d. all of the above are true

15. The most important determinant of interference is _____.
    a. similarity
    b. complexity
    c. decay
    d. rehearsal time

16. In interviewing witnesses to a bank robbery, a detective hears a different story from each witness. Witnesses recall different hair color, height, and even the number of suspects involved. The most likely explanation for these differences in the stories of the witnesses is _____.
    a. retroactive interference
    b. proactive interference
    c. eidetic imagery
    d. reconstructive memory

17. A type of memory loss that has no known neurological cause is called

    _____.
    a. proactive amnesia
    b. retrograde amnesia
    c. eidetic
    d. hysterical amnesia

Answers and Explanations to Multiple Choice Pretest

1. c. Forgetting occurs rapidly at first and then levels off. This is the reason you should review material often.

2. d. Overlearning is continuing to study information after you know it.

3. a. Sensory register receives sensory information from the external world.

4. c. Attention is the process of selective looking, listening, smelling and feeling.

5. d. Working memory is the same as short-term memory.

6. b. New research indicates that short-term memory can hold what is rehearsed for 1.5 to 2.0 seconds.

7. d. Chunking is grouping information.

8. d. Information remains in short-term memory for 15-20 seconds.

9. b. Rote rehearsal is repeating something over and over again to retain it in short-term memory.

10. c. Elaborative rehearsal connects new information with familiar information already in long-term memory.

11. d. Long-term memory is relatively permanent, although it sometimes experiences decay or interference.

12. c. Semantic memory stores facts.

13. d. Episodic memory stores information with personal meaning.

14. c. The setting you learning in provides retrieval cues.

15. a. Similarity of material can lead to greater amounts of interference.

16. d. Eye witness testimony is subject to reconstructive memory.

17. d. Hysterical amnesia is memory loss with no neurological cause.

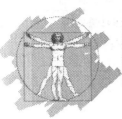

Learning Objectives

After you have read and studied this chapter, you should be able to complete the following statements. Your exam is written based on these learning objectives.

1. Describe the path information takes from the environment to long-term memory.

2. Explain the characteristics of short-term and long-term memory.

3. Explain coding in both short-term and long-term memory.

4. Outline storage and retrieval in long-term memory.

5. Discuss explanations for forgetting.

6. Describe the different types of memory, and their characteristic properties.

7. Know the limits of memory and determine if they can be expanded.

8. Describe how information is stored and how it is organized.

9. Define "schema". How are schemata used?

10. Discuss how and why memories change over time.

11. Understand and use techniques for improving your memory.

12. Describe and explain the brain structures and regions that are the bases for memory.

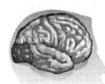

Short Essay Questions

Write out your answers to the following eight essay questions to further your mastery of the topics.

1. What three processes are involved in the act of remembering?

_____

_____

_____

_____

_____

_____

_____

_____

_____

2. What are the characteristics of short-term memory?

_____

_____

_____

_____

_____

_____

_____

_____

3. What are the three methods of measuring retention?

_____

_____

_____

_____

_____

_____

_____

_____

_____

4. Explain Ebbinghaus' contribution to psychology. _____

_____

_____

_____

_____

_____

_____

_____

5. What are six causes of forgetting?

_____

_____

_____

_____

_____

_____

_____

_____

_____

_____

_____

_____

6. What is interference and how can it be minimized?

_____

_____

_____

_____

_____

_____

_____

_____

_____

_____

_____

7. What is the state-dependent memory effect?

_____

_____

_____

_____

_____

_____

_____

_____

_____

_____

_____

_____

8. What are four study habits that can aid memory?

_____

_____

_____

_____

_____

_____

_____

_____

_____

_____

_____

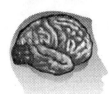

Language Support

Students identified the following words from the text as needing more explanation. This page can be cut-out, folded in half, and used as a bookmark for this chapter.

A
acoustically — related to sound
apparent — obvious
articulate — speaks well
astonished — surprised

B
barring — stopping
burglar — someone who steals

C
captured — caught
cluster — group together
concussion — injury from a hit on the head

D
digit — number
disoriented — confused
disruptions — things that get in the way
disrupts — keeps in the way of
dissimilar — not the same
doggedly — do not give up
eluded — got past him

E
enormity — large size
entirely — completely
extract — get out
extraordinary — very good

F
fallibility — ability to be wrong

I
icon — picture
inadvertently — happen by mistake
interferes with — gets in the way
interrupted — stopped before finished

L
larcenous — evil

M
melodramatic — very dramatic story
mentioned — stated

O
oblivious — does not notice
overlearning — studying more than is needed

P
pay attention — focus
podium or lectern — a stand for speaker notes

P
predominantly	mainly
pronounced	noticeable

R
rambling story	story that goes on too long and does not follow a logical path
relevance	importance which is directly related
retrieve	get it back
retrieving	getting back

S
senseless trivia	information of very little importance
simultaneously	at the same time
subsequent	coming after
swerved	vehicle, such as a car, moves quickly to one side

V
vividly	very clearly

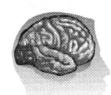

Multiple Choice Posttest

After studying the text and completing the Study Guide activities, answer these questions to determine if you need to review any areas before the course exam.

1. Researchers have shown that overlearning _____.
   a. has no appreciable positive or negative effect on memorization of material
   b. increases short-term but not long-term retention of material
   c. increases both short-term and long-term retention of material
   d. often causes people to confuse information and lowers their accurate retention of that material

2. Our visual sensation of a classmate walking past us would initially be in the _____.
   a. sensory registers
   b. short-term memory
   c. long-term memory
   d. hippocampus

3. Chunking is a means of _____.
   a. storing long-term memories
   b. immediately forgetting irrelevant details
   c. arranging details into a hierarchy from most to least important
   d. organizing information into meaningful units

4. According to the _____ theory, information gets pushed aside or confused by other information in short-term memory.
   a. interference
   b. distractor
   c. stimulus-response
   d. decay

5. Elaborative rehearsal involves _____.
   a. repeating something as well as physically acting out the concept you are trying to learn
   b. organizing basic information into meaningful units
   c. repeating something over and over again
   d. relating new information to something you already know

6. The portion of long-term memory that stores general facts and information is called _____.
   a. eidetic
   b. episodic
   c. semantic
   d. procedural

7. An item is easier to remember _____.
   a. if it is stored in short-term memory
   b. if it is part of our episodic memory
   c. the more connections it has with information already in long-term memory
   d. all of the above are true

8. While memorizing a list of words, students are exposed to the smell of garlic. If the students recall more words when there is the smell of garlic, then the effect of garlic is most likely due to _____ memory.
   a. explicit
   b. implicit
   c. procedural
   d. eidetic

9. Proactive interference of long-term memory means _____.
   a. old material has eliminated memories of new material
   b. old material interferes with remembering new material
   c. new material represses short-term memories
   d. new material interferes with remembering old material

10. When memories are not lost but are transformed into something somewhat different, it is called _____.
    a. retroactive interference
    b. eidetic memory
    c. proactive interference
    d. reconstructive memory

11. Our recollection of events that occurred in our life and when those events took place is called _____ memory.
    a. autobiographical
    b. reconstructive
    c. semantic
    d. procedural

12. Memories that concern events that are highly significant and are vividly remembered are called _____.
    a. eyewitness images
    b. flashbulb memories
    c. elaborative rehearsals
    d. eidetic images

13. Eidetic imagery is sometimes called _____.
    a. a mnemonic device
    b. an echo
    c. semantic memory
    d. photographic memory

14. We use mnemonics to _____.
    a. block out information that is not consistent with our viewpoint
    b. block out information that is painful
    c. give order to information we want to learn
    d. block out information that is useless

15. The hippocampus is important for _____.
    a. transferring information from short-term to long-term memory
    b. the retrieval of memories from long-term memory
    c. maintaining a constant level of attention
    d. the formation of short-term memory

16. A form of amnesia related to alcoholism is _____.
    a. Alzheimer's disease
    b. Milner's syndrome
    c. Korsakoff's syndrome
    d. Wernicke's syndrome

17. _____ memory tends to improve with age.
    a. Implict
    b. Eidetic
    c. Episodic
    d. Semantic

Answers and Explanations to Multiple Choice Posttest

1. c. Overlearning increases both short-term and long-term memory.
2. a. Visual sensations are stored in sensory memory.
3. d. Chunking is organizing information into groups.
4. a. Interference results when information gets pushed aside by other information.
5. d. Elaborative Rehearsal relates new information to something we already know.
6. c. Semantic memory stores general information.
7. c. An item is easier to remember if we connect it to things already in long-term memory.
8. b. Implicit memory provides retrieval cues.
9. b. Old material interfering with remembering new material is called proactive interference.
10. d. Reconstructive memory changes the original memory.
11. a. Autobiographical memory is our collection of memories for event which took place in our lives.
12. b. We have flashbulb memories for certain important events in our lives
13. d. Eidetic imagery is the same as photographic memory.
14. c. Mnemonics give order to information we want to learn.
15. a. Hippocampus is important to convert short-term into long-term memory.
16. c. Wernicke's syndrome may include amnesia and is due to alcoholism.
17. d. Semantic memory increases with age as we get wiser.

Key Vocabulary Terms

Cut-out each term and use as study cards.
Definition is on the backside of each term.

Sensory registers	Elaborative rehearsal
Attention	Retrograde anmesia
Short-term memory (STM)	Long-term memory (LTM)
Chunking	Semantic memory
Decay theory	Episodic memory
Interference theory	Explicit memory
Rote rehearsal	Implicit memory

The linking of new information in short-term memory to familiar material stored in long-term memory.	Entry points for raw information from the senses.
Inability to recall events immediately preceding an accident or injury, but without loss of earlier memory.	Selection of some incoming information for further processing.
Portion of memory that is more or less permanent and that corresponds to everything we "know."	Working memory; briefly stores and processes selected information from the sensory registers.
Portion of long-term memory that stores general facts and information.	Grouping of information into meaningful units for easier handling by short-term memory.
Portion of long-term memory that stores more specific information that has personal meaning.	A theory that argues that the passage of time itself causes forgetting.
Memory for information that was intentionally committed to memory or intentionally retrieved from memory.	A theory that argues that interference from other information causes forgetting.
Memory for information that either was unintentionally committed to memory or was unintentionally retrieved from memory.	Retaining information in STM simply by repeating it over and over.

Retroactive interference	
Proactive interference	
Schema	
Flashbulb memory	
Eidetic imagery	
Mnemonist	
Mnemonics	

	Process by which new information interferes with old information already in memory.
	Process by which old material already in memory interferes with new information.
	Set of beliefs or expectation about something that is based on past experience.
	A vivid memory of a certain event and the incidents surrounding it even after a long time has passed.
	The ability to reproduce unusually sharp and detailed images of something that has been seen.
	Someone with highly developed memory skills.
	Techniques that make material easier to remember.

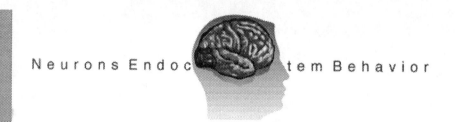

Neurons Endoc tem Behavior

Overview

● ●

Building Blocks of Thought
Language
Images
Concepts

Problem Solving
The Interpretation of Problems
Producing and Evaluating Solutions
Obstacles to Solving Problems
Becoming Better at Problem Solving

Decision Making

Language and Thought

Intelligence

Formal Theories of Intelligence

Intelligence Tests
The Stanford-Binet Intelligence Scale
The Wechsler Intelligence Scales
Group Tests
Performance and Culture-fair Tests

What Makes a Good Test?
Reliability
Validity
Criticisms of IQ Tests

Determinants of Intelligence
Heredity
Environment
The IQ Debate: A Continuing
Controversy

Extremes of Intelligence
Mental Retardation
Giftedness

Creativity

COGNITION AND MENTAL ABILITIES

7

Class and Text Notes

This outline provides a way to organize your notes from both the text and the lecture. It will also serve as review sheets for the exam.

Building Blocks of Thought

Language

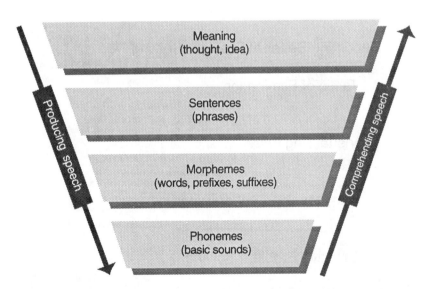

Images

Concepts

Decision Making

Compensatory model

Noncompensatory model

Representativeness

Availability

Confirmation bias

Language and Thought

Linguistic relativity hypothesis

Figurative language

Intelligence

Formal Theories of Intelligence

Spearman

Thurstone

Sternberg

Compential intelligence

Experiential intelligence

Contextual intelligence

Gardner - theory of multiple intelligences

Intelligence Tests

The Stanford-Binet Intelligence Scale

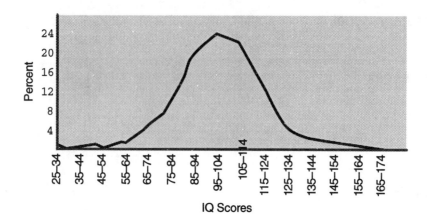

The Wechsler Intelligence Scales

Group Tests

Performance and Culture-fair Tests

What Makes a Good Test?

Reliability

Validity

Criticisms of IQ Tests

Determinants of Intelligence

Heredity

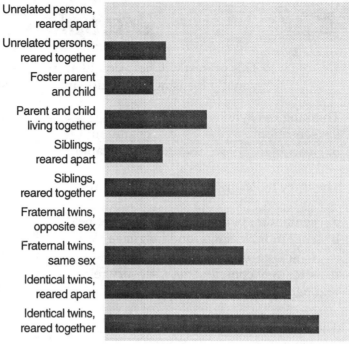

Unrelated persons, reared apart

Unrelated persons, reared together

Foster parent and child

Parent and child living together

Siblings, reared apart

Siblings, reared together

Fraternal twins, opposite sex

Fraternal twins, same sex

Identical twins, reared apart

Identical twins, reared together

.10 .20 .30 .40 .50 .60 .70 .80 .90 1.
Correlations of IQs

Environment

The IQ Debate: A Continuing Controversy

Extremes of Intelligence

Mental Retardation

Giftedness

Creativity

Multiple Choice Pretest

This pretest will help you identify the topics in the chapter that are most difficult for you. By focusing your study time in those areas, you will see the greatest improvement.

1. Thinking is a synonym for _____.
   a. sensation
   b. learning
   c. cognition
   d. organization

2. The three building blocks of thought are _____.
   a. semantics, phonemes, and morphemes
   b. cognition, feelings, and language
   c. language, images, and concepts
   d. stream of consciousness, sensory registry, and perception

3. The sounds of "th," "ch," and "ph" are _____.
   a. semantics
   b. syntax
   c. morphemes
   d. phonemes

4. The ability to adjust to new tasks and situations, to gain insights, and to adapt creatively involves _____ intelligence, according to Sternberg.
   a. exponential
   b. componential
   c. experiential
   d. contextual

5. The language rules that determine how sounds and words can be combined and used to communicate meaning within a language are collectively known as _____.
   a. semantics
   b. syntax
   c. morphemes
   d. grammar

6. Most concepts that people use in thinking _____.
   a. accurately account for critical differences among various images
   b. depend on the magnitude of sensory memory
   c. allow them to generalize but not to think abstractly
   d. are fuzzy and overlap with one another

7. A mental model containing the most typical features of a concept is called a(n)
   a. algorithm
   b. prototype
   c. stereotype
   d. description

8. Our conception of events as we think they will probably be is called _____.
   a. a noncompensatory model
   b. a compensatory model
   c. an idealized cognitive model
   d. a prototype

9. Many people fail to solve the "pieces of chain" problem or the "six matches" problem discussed in the text because _____.
   a. they develop conceptual blocks resulting from overly rigid assumptions
   b. they use an incorrect algorithm
   c. they use heuristic methods rather than trial and error
   d. they use hill-climbing instead of creating subgoals

10. Successive elimination of incorrect solutions to problems until the correct solution is found is called the _____ problem-solving strategy.
    a. heuristics
    b. trial and error
    c. hill-climbing
    d. information retrieval

11. The problem-solving methods that guarantee a solution are called _____.
    a. heuristics
    b. trial and error
    c. hill-climbing
    d. algorithms

12. Rules of thumb that do not guarantee a solution but may help bring one within reach are called _____.
    a. heuristics
    b. trial and error
    c. hill-climbing
    d. information retrieval

13. It is starting to rain and there is a very high window that is wide open. Jamie is upset because the rain is falling on her piano but she does not think to use the long handle of a broom to close the window. Jamie is exhibiting the problem of _____.
    a. inadequate means-end analysis
    b. working backward
    c. functional fixedness
    d. noncompensatory modeling

14. Huan doesn't know where he wants to go to college but he does know he does not want to live where there is snow. He should use the problem solving technique of _____ to narrow down his choices of colleges.
    a. means-end analysis
    b. working backward
    c. locational analysis
    d. elimination

15. Research indicates that a novice can often outperform an expert _____.
    a. in situations that require the ability to use information in large, interconnected "chunks"
    b. when rigid, linear thinking is necessary to solve the problem
    c. when a novel or creative solution to a problem is required
    d. when it is crucial to recognize all the facts of a complex situation

16. A technique that encourages a group to generate a list of ideas without evaluation is called
    _____.
    a. convergent thinking
    b. brainstorming
    c. circular thinking
    d. functional thinking

17. Jennifer went to buy a car. She really wanted a red car but there was a great price on a blue car which had a lot of expensive equipment on it that she wanted. Jennifer used the _____ decision making style when she decided to buy the blue car.
    a. compensatory model
    b. means-end analysis
    c. noncompensatory model
    d. functional analysis

Answers and Explanations to Multiple Choice Pretest

1. c.
2. c. Language, images, and concepts are important components of thought.
3. d.
4. c.
5. d.
6. d.
7. b.
8. c.
9. a. Problem solving can fail if rigid assumptions interfere with our ability to approach new problems in a flexible way.
10. b.
11. d.
12. a.
13. c. Functional fixedness is seeing only one use for something.
14. d. Huan can narrow down his choices by eliminating those areas in which he knows he would not live.
15. c. Experts can sometimes be so focused on their knowledge of the situation that they miss the creative solutions.
16. b.
17. a. Jennifer used the compensation model of decision making because the blue car's extra equipment and good price compensated for it not being red.

Learning Objectives

After you have read and studied this chapter, you should be able to complete the following statements. Your exam is written based on these learning objectives.

1. Define phonemes and morphemes.

2. Define grammar and its components.

3. Distinguish between the concepts of "surface structure" and "deep structure."

4. Define cognition. Differentiate between images and concepts. Explain the use of prototypes.

5. Describe the basic steps of problem-solving. List and describe the four types of solution strategies.

6. Discuss various obstacles to problem-solving.

7. Describe four ways in which a person can become a better problem solver. Distinguish between divergent and convergent thinking.

8. Compare two models of decision-making and explain why one leads to a better solution than the other.

9. Distinguish between heuristics and algorithms.

10. Summarize the relationship between language and thinking. Explain Whorf's linguistic relativity hypothesis. Cite criticisms of Whorf's hypothesis.

11. Summarize the views of Spearman, Thurstone, Guilford, and Cattell with respect to what constitutes intelligence.

12. Trace the development of intelligence tests from Binet through Terman, noting the contributions of each. Describe the standard procedure for the Stanford-Binet Scale.

13. Distinguish the Wechsler Adult Intelligence Scale-Revised from the Stanford-Binet. Identify the two parts of the WAIS-R.

14. Distinguish between individual and group tests. Give three examples of group tests. List the advantages and disadvantages of group tests.

15. Describe the purposes of performance tests and culture-fair tests.

16. Define reliability and validity. Identify three techniques for measuring reliability and validity.

17. Identify four criticisms of IQ tests. Distinguish between IQ scores and intelligence.

18. Explain the high correlation between IQ scores and academic.

19. Explain the relationship between gender differences and cognitive abilities.

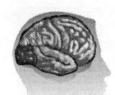

Short Essay Questions

Write out your answers to the following four essay questions to further your mastery of the topics.

1. Explain the goals and results of the Little Albert study. Also explain desensitization.

_____

_____

_____

_____

_____

_____

_____

_____

_____

_____

2. What are conceptual blocks and how do they inhibit effective problem solving?

_____

_____

_____

_____

_____

_____

_____

_____

_____

_____

3. Identify and compare four different problem-solving strategies and list the advantages and disadvantages of each strategy.

_____

_____

_____

_____

_____

_____

_____

_____

_____

_____

4. Compare and contrast divergent and convergent thinking. Discuss their role in creative problem solving, as well as brainstorming.

_____

_____

_____

_____

_____

_____

_____

_____

_____

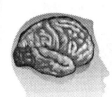

Language Support

Students identified the following words from the text as needing more explanation. This page can be cut-out, folded in half, and used as a bookmark for this chapter.

A
arbitrary — without much thought before
assimilated — taken into
astronauts — people who fly to other planets and the moon.
astronomer — a person who studies the stars, planets, and moons.

B
batter — the person in the game of baseball who hits the ball
blackboard — old name for board a teacher writes on; typically it is white or green

C
clarify — to make clear and understandable
clear-cut — easily understood
collide — hit
combat — fighting
compassionate — caring
composed — make up
conceding — giving
conceive — thinks up
constraints — limits
construct — make
contend — state a belief
criterion — guideline or standard

D
deliberate — on purpose
deteriorate — break down
detours — turn away from the direct route
disconfirming evidence — information that does not agree
dispute — disagreement

E
ensured — make sure it happens
equilateral — having the same length sides on all three sides
established — set up in advance
exhaust — smoke an engine puts out when it is running
experimentation — trying many different things
extensively — thoroughly
extraordinary genius — very high level of intelligence
extraterrestrial — a living organism from another planet

F
figurative language — words which only serve as an example
fostering — encouraging, helping

H
hamper — get in the way of
hinder — get in the way of
hindsight — understanding something clearly but after it has happened

I
invent   make up
K
keenly developed   well developed
knack   special ability
linguistic   related to language
M
minimizing   make smaller
modify   change
noncompensatory   do not make up for
N
nonetheless   however
novice   someone who is new at something
O
obvious   easily seen
optimal   the best
overcrowding   too many in a small space
P
parentheses   "(   )"
perform   do
potentially   possibly
pouring rain   heavy rain
predetermined   known before
R
rages   goes on with great energy
relevant   has meaning and importance
rich assortment   many different types
rigid   firm
rules of thumb   a set of rules to follow
S
self-reliance   relying on oneself
shortcomings   problems
shortsighted   not seeing the whole picture
shrewd   smart
step-by-step   carefully following a plan
strategy   plan
suspending   stopping
T
tactic   planned way of doing something
tangled   confused
trivial   not important
U
unambiguous   clear
W
wide range   many different

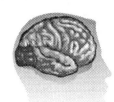

Multiple Choice Posttest

After studying the text and completing the Study Guide activities, answer these questions to determine if you need to review any areas before the course exam.

1. _____ tests measure a person's mental ability.
   a. Aptitude
   b. Social competence
   c. Apperception
   d. Intelligence

2. Tests designed to predict a person's future achievement in a specific area are called _____ tests.
   a. aptitude
   b. social competence
   c. apperception
   d. intelligence

3. The abilities involved in learning and adaptive behavior are usually labelled as _____.
   a. aptitude
   b. social competence
   c. apperception
   d. intelligence

4. The ability to focus on one's strengths, compensate for weaknesses, and seek out environments in which one can function most effectively reflect _____ intelligence, according to Sternberg.
   a. exponential
   b. componential
   c. experiential
   d. contextual

5. Gardner's approach to intelligence emphasizes _____.
   a. underlying generalized intelligence
   b. the unique abilities of each individual
   c. skills required in school
   d. physical skills

6. According to Binet's test, a child who scores as well as an 8-year-old has the _____ of 8.
   a. content validity
   b. basal age
   c. mental age
   d. aptitude

7. Which individual test is most often given to adults?
   a. MMPI
   b. Stanford-Binet
   c. WAIS-R
   d. WISC-R

8. The WAIS-R measures _____; whereas, the Stanford-Binet does not.
   a. verbal skills
   b. integration skills
   c. perceptual skills
   d. performance skills

9. The ability of a test to produce consistent and stable scores is its _____.
   a. validity
   b. standard deviation
   c. standardization
   d. reliability

10. The degree of association between two variables can be shown with a statistical measure called a _____.
    a. correlational coefficient
    b. experimental factor
    c. level of significance
    d. progressive matrices

11. A test that is valid measures _____.
    a. consistent results
    b. split-half reliability
    c. what it sets out to measure
    d. subjectivity

12. When an employment test accurately predicts how well someone will do on specific measures of important job related skills, the test is showing good _____ validity.
    a. split-half
    b. criterion-related
    c. content
    d. performance

13. What are predictors of occupational success?
    a. IQ scores, but not school grades
    b. school grades, but not IQ scores
    c. neither IQ scores nor school grades
    d. test scores

14. The idea that heredity affects IQ is MOST supported by the high correlation between IQ scores of _____.
    a. fraternal twins reared together
    b. fraternal twins reared apart
    c. identical twins reared together
    d. identical twins reared apart

15. In the United States, the _____ Program is a large nationwide program designed to help educationally disadvantaged children.
    a. Westgate
    b. Head Start
    c. Milwaukee
    d. Stanford-Binet

16. The average IQ scores is _____.
    a. 80   c. 120
    b. 100   d. 160

17. A disorder called _____ results in mental retardation and characteristic physical deformities on the hands, feet, and eyelids.
    a. PKU
    b. fragile-X syndrome
    c. hemophilia
    d. Down syndrome

18. Each of the following is a required procedure of the Education for All Handicapped Children Act of 1975 EXCEPT _____.
    a. a team of specialists must determine each child's educational needs
    b. handicapped children must be tested to identify their disabilities
    c. an educational program that meets the child's needs must be provided
    d. children must be mainstreamed, no matter what their disability

19. Each of the following has been shown to interfere with creativity EXCEPT
    a. rejecting parents
    b. performing on command
    c. mild mood swings
    d. competition

Answers and Explanations to Multiple Choice Posttest

1. d.
2. a.
3. d.
4. d.
5. b. Gardner's theory of intelligence emphasizes the seven abilities of
6. c.
7. c.
8. d. The WAIS-R measures both verbal ability and performance.
9. d.
10. a.
11. c.
12. b. Criterion-related validity examines how closely the test results relate to a separate measure in a specific area.
13. c.
14. d.
15. b. The Head Start program focuses on providing a stimulating environment for preschool children age 3-5. The program has been shown to help the child achieve better in school.
16. b.
17. d.
18. d.
19. c. Creativity can be inhibited by competition, performing on command (being told to "creative now"), and rejecting parents.

Key Vocabulary Terms

Cut-out each term and use as study cards.
Definition is on the backside of each term.

Cognition	Syntax
Phonemes	Image
Morphemes	Concept
Surface structure	Prototype
Deep structure	Idealized cognitive model
Grammar	Ad hoc categories
Semantics	Problem representation

The rules for arranging words into grammatical sentences.	The process whereby we acquire and use knowledge.
A mental representation of a sensory experience.	The basic sounds that make up any language.
A mental category for classifying object, people, or experiences.	The smallest meaningful units of speech, such as simple words, prefixes, and suffixes.
According to Rosch, a mental model containing the most typical feature of a concept.	The particular words and phrases used to make up a sentence.
Our conception of events as we expect to typically find them.	The underlying meaning of a sentence.
Novel concepts created for a special purpose or occasion.	The language rules that determine how sounds and words can be combined and used to communicate meaning within a language.
The first step in solving a problem; it involves interpreting or defining the problem.	The criteria for assigning meaning to the morphemes in a language.

Trial and error	Working backward
Information retrieval	Set
Algorithm	Functional fixedness
Heuristics	Tactic of elimination
Hill climbing	Visualizing
Subgoals	Divergent thinking
Means-end analysis	Convergent thinking

A heuristic strategy in which one works backward from the desired goal to the given conditions.

A problem-solving strategy based on the successive elimination of incorrect solutions until the correct one is found.

Tendency to perceive and to approach problems in certain ways.

A problem-solving strategy that requires only the recovery of information from long-term memory.

The tendency to perceive only a limited number of uses for an object, thus interfering with the process of problem solving.

A step-by-step method of problem solving that guarantees a correct solution.

A problem-solving strategy in which possible solutions are evaluated according to appropriate criteria and discarded as they fail to contribute to a solution.

Rules of thumb that help in simplifying and solving problems, although they do not guarantee a correct solution.

A problem-solving strategy in which principals or concepts are drawn, diagrammed, or charted so that they can be better understood.

A heuristic problem- solving strategy in which each step moves you progressively closer to the final goal.

Thinking that meets the criteria of originality, inventiveness, and flexibility.

Intermediate, more manageable goals used in one heuristic strategy to make it easier to reach the final goal.

Thinking that is directed toward a correct solution to a problem.

A heuristic strategy that aims to reduce the discrepancy between the current situation and the desired goal at a number of intermediate points.

Brainstorming	Figurative language
Compensatory model	Intelligence tests
Noncompensatory model	Intelligence
Representative	Operations
Availability	Contents
Confirmation bias	Products
Linguistic reality hypothesis	Triarchic theory of intelligence

Expressive or nonliteral language such as metaphor and irony.	A problem-solving strategy in which an individual or a group produces numerous ideas and evaluates them only after all ideas have been collected.
Tests designed to measure a person's general mental abilities.	A rational decision-making model in which choices are systematically evaluated on various criteria.
A general term referring to the ability or abilities involved in learning and adaptive behavior.	A decision-making model in which weakness in one or more criteria are not offset by strengths in other criteria.
According to Guilford, the act of thinking.	A heuristic by which a new situation is judged on the basis of its resemblance to a stereo-typical model.
According to Guilford, the terms we use in thinking, such as words or symbols.	A heuristic by which a judgment or decision is based on information that is most easily retrieved from memory.
According to Guilford, the ideas that result from thinking.	The tendency to look for evidence in support of a belief and to ignore evidence that would disprove a belief.
Sternberg's theory that intelligence involves mental skills, insight and creative adaptability, and environmental responsiveness.	Whorf's idea that patterns of thinking are determined by the specific language one speaks.

Componential intelligence	Wechsler Adult Intelligence Scale
Experiential intelligence	Wechsler Scale for Children
Contextual intelligence	Group test
Theory of multiple intelligences	Performance tests
Binet-Simon Scale	Culture-fair tests
Intelligence quotient (IQ)	Reliability
Stanford-Binet Intelligence Scale	Split-half reliability

Individual intelligence test developed especially for adults; measures both verbal and performance abilities.	According to Sternberg, the ability to acquire new knowledge, to solve problems effectively.
Individual intelligence test developed especially for school-aged children; measures verbal and performance abilities and also yields an overall IQ score.	Accordingly to Sternberg, the ability to adapt creatively in new situations, to use insight.
Written intelligence tests administered by one examiner to many people at one time.	According to Sternberg, the ability to select contexts in which you can excel, to shape the environment to fit your strengths.
Intelligence tests that minimize the use of language.	Howard Gardner's theory that there is not one intelligence, but rather many intelligences, each of which is relatively independent of the others.
Intelligence tests designed to eliminate cultural bias by minimizing skills and values that vary from one culture to another.	The first test of intelligence, developed for testing children.
Ability of a test to produce consistent and stable scores.	A numerical value given to intelligence that is determined from the scores on an intelligence test; based on a score of 100 for average intelligence.
A method of determining test reliability by dividing the test into two parts and checking the agreement of scores on both parts.	Terman's adaptation of the Binet-Simon Scale.

Correlation coefficients	Creativity
Validity	
Content validity	
Criterion-related validity	
Tacit knowledge	
Mental retardation	
Giftedness	

The ability to produce novel and unique socially valued ideas or objects.	Statistical measures of the degree of association between two variables.
	Ability of a test to measure what it has been designed to measure .
	Refers to a test's having an adequate sample of the skills or knowledge it is supposed to measure.
	Validity of a test as measured by a comparison of the test score and independent measures of that which the test is designed to measure.
	Knowledge one needs for success on particular particle tasks, which may not be explicit.
	Condition of significantly subaverage intelligence combined with defenses in adaptive behavior.
	Refers to superior IQ combined with demonstrated or potential ability in such areas as academic aptitude, creativity, or leadership.

Neurons Endocrine System Behavior

Overview

● ●

LIFE SPAN DEVELOPMENT

8

This outline provides a way to organize your notes from both the text and the lecture. It will also serve as review sheets for the exam.

Prenatal Development

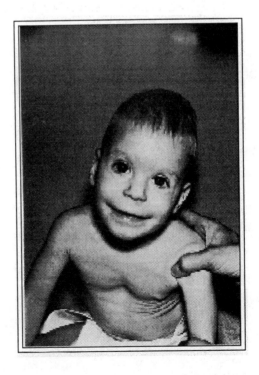

The Newborn Baby

Reflexes

Temperament

The Perceptual Abilities of Infants

Infancy and Childhood

Physical Development

Motor Development

Cognitive Development

Moral Development

Language Development

Social Development

Relationships with Other Children

Television and Children

Adolescence

Physical Changes

Cognitive Changes

Personality and Social Development

Problems of Adolescence

Adulthood

Love, Partnerships, and Parenting

The World of Work

Cognitive Changes

Personality Changes

The "Change of Life"

Late Adulthood

Physical Changes

Social Development

Retirement

Sexual Behavior

Cognitive Changes

Facing the End of Life

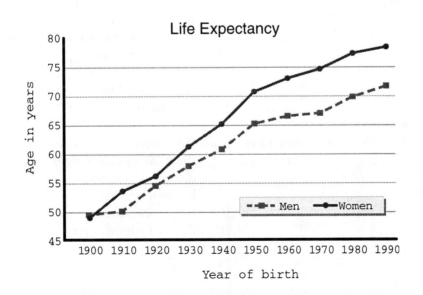

Life Expectancy

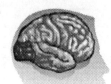

Multiple Choice Pretest

This pretest will help you identify the topics in the chapter that are most difficult for you. By focusing your study time in those areas, you will see the greatest improvement.

1. A health psychologist is interested in determining if an inability to cope with stress during adolescence is correlated with an inability to cope with stress in adulthood. She assesses coping skills in a group of 100 adolescents and then contacts the same people 10 years later. This is a _____ study.
   a. experimental
   b. cross-sectional
   c. longitudinal
   d. biographical

2. When a sample of people of various ages are part of a research study done at one point in time, this study is utilizing the _____ method.
   a. experimental
   b. cross-sectional
   c. longitudinal
   d. biographical

3. A group of people born during the same period of historical time is called _____.
   a. a cohort
   b. a peerage
   c. a cross-sectional group
   d. a convergent group

4. The _____ period of development is from conception to birth.
   a. natal
   b. zygote
   c. embryo
   d. prenatal

5. The structure that attaches a fetus to its mother's uterus and provides nourishment is called the _____.
   a. amniotic sac
   b. fallopian tube
   c. placenta
   d. structuralism

6. A child has facial deformities, heart defects, cognitive impairments, and stunted growth. The child likely suffers from _____.
   a. prematurity
   b. fetal alcohol syndrome
   c. contact deficiencies
   d. none of the above

7. Rachel is a strong willed child, who is moody and intense. She often throws temper tantrums, and adapts poorly to change. Thomas and Chess would say her temperament is _____.
   a. difficult
   b. predictable
   c. easy
   d. slow-to-warm-up

8. Jean Piaget is most famous for his theory of _____ development.
   a. moral
   b. motor
   c. language
   d. cognitive

9. Which of the following is the correct order for Piaget's four stages of development?
   a. preoperational, sensory-motor, concrete operations, formal operation
   b. concrete operations, preoperational, sensory-motor, formal operation
   c. sensory-motor, preoperational, concrete operations, formal operation
   d. preoperational, concrete operations, sensory-motor, formal operation

10. An individual who perceives everything from their own perceptive is exhibiting _____.
    a. conservation
    b. ethnocentrism
    c. egocentrism
    d. anthropomorphism

11. Lawrence Kohlberg developed a theory of
_____.
   a. cognitive development
   b. correlational coefficients
   c. longitudinal research
   d. moral development

12. Conflicts over what is moral and what is legal
are likely to occur during the _____ level
of moral thinking.
   a. concrete operational
   b. preconventional
   c. conventional
   d. postconventional

13. Researchers who study language development
in deaf children who have deaf parents have
found that the children _____.
   a. babble with their hands
   b. do not babble at all
   c. babble like other infants for a short while,
      but quickly stop
   d. babble verbally

14. The process of _____ teaches children
what behaviors and attitudes are appropriate
in their family, friends, and culture.
   a. attachment
   b. imprinting
   c. socialization
   d. autonomy

15. Authoritarian parents are to _____ children
as permissive parents are to _____ children.
   a. distrustful; assertive   b. passive;
   assertive
   c. inquisitive; withdrawn
   d. distrustful; dependent

16. _____ is knowing what behavior is
appropriate for each gender.
   a. Gender constancy
   b. Gender awareness
   c. Sex-role awareness
   d. Innate behavior patterns

17. Other than sleeping, children spend the most
time _____.
   a. in school
   b. watching TV
   c. playing with toys
   d. playing with friends

Answers and Explanations to Multiple Choice Pretest

1. c. Longitudinal research studies the same people over a long period of time.

2. b. Cross-sectional research studies people of different ages at one point in time.

3. a.

4 d.

5. c.

6. b. Fetal alcohol result when the mother of the fetus consumers too much alcohol.

7. a. Thomas and Chess states that a percentage of children can be classified as difficult.

8. d.

9. c.

10. c. Egocentrism is seeing everything from one's own perspective.

11. d.

12. d. Postconventional moral reasoning focuses on principles such as justice, liberty, and equality.

13. a.

14. c.

15. d.

16. c.

17. b.

Learning Objectives

After you have read and studied this chapter, you should be able to complete the following statements. Your exam is written based on these learning objectives.

1. Describe the prenatal environment.

2. Describe the physical and motor development of the newborn baby.

3. Describe the perceptual development of a baby. How does object perception change?

4. What are some of the factors influencing depth perception in infants?

5. What are the four stages of Piaget's theory of cognitive development?

6. List four factors associated with the social development of a child.

7. Trace language development from infancy through age 5 or 6.

8. Explain the critical periods in language development.

9. Explain the importance of secure attachments between a caregiver and child.

10. Describe how children learn such values as friendship.

11. Explain how sex-role identity is formed.

12. Summarize the important physical changes that the adolescent undergoes during puberty.

13. Describe the cognitive development of adolescents.

14. Describe the sequence of social development from the start of adolescence though young adulthood.

15. Discuss four problems of adolescence: self-esteem, depression, suicide, and eating disorders.

16. Distinguish between the longitudinal and cross-sectional methods as they relate to the study of adulthood. List the disadvantages of the methods and how the disadvantages can be overcome.

17. Identify the central concerns and crises that characterize the young, middle, and late adulthood stages.

18. Summarize the physiological changes that people undergo as they age.

19. Identify the changes in cognitive development that people undergo as they age.

20. Summarize the differences in the ways men and women in young, middle, and later adulthood approach friendship, marriage, sexuality, parenthood, divorce, death of a spouse, and work.

21. List the factors that influence attitudes toward retirement.

22. Identify Elisabeth Kubler-Ross' five sequential stages though which people pass as they react to their own impending death.

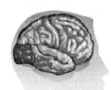

Short Essay Questions

Write out your answers to the following eight essay questions to further your mastery of the topics.

1. Compare and contrast the longitudinal, crossectional, and biographical approaches to studying development in adulthood.

_____

_____

_____

_____

_____

_____

_____

_____

_____

_____

_____

_____

2. Define maturation and discuss the factors that affect it.

_____

_____

_____

_____

_____

_____

_____

_____

_____

_____

_____

3. Explain Kohlberg's theory of moral development. What are some criticisms of Kohlberg's theory?

_____

_____

_____

_____

_____

_____

_____

_____

_____

_____

_____

_____

4. Compare and contrast the major theories of language development in children.

_____

_____

_____

_____

_____

_____

_____

_____

_____

_____

_____

5. Discuss Piaget's four stages of cognitive development.

_____

_____

_____

_____

_____

_____

_____

_____

_____

_____

6. Discuss the impact of bilingualism on the language and learning abilities of children.

_____

_____

_____

_____

_____

_____

_____

_____

_____

_____

7. Describe the effects of divorce on adults.

_____

_____

_____

_____

_____

_____

_____

_____

_____

_____

8. Explain Levinson's theory of adult development.

_____

_____

_____

_____

_____

_____

_____

_____

_____

_____

_____

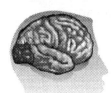

Language Support

Students identified the following words from the text as needing more explanation. This page can be cut-out, folded in half, and used as a bookmark for this chapter.

A
abrupt	sudden
accustomed	used to
acquisition	to gain or acquire
alleviating	get rid of; stop
approaches	different ways of doing things
aspirations	future goals and dreams
assumption	to believe
attributed	state the cause of
autonomy	to work alone

C
chaos	confusion
checkerboard	a pattern in cloth of light and dark small squares
cling	hang on to
colleagues	coworkers
congenital	happen during fetal development
criminal behavior	actions which break the law

D
dashing	hurting
depersonalization	not treated with the respect a person should receive
devastating	very bad
dictates	demands
dimension	aspect; part
disastrous	very bad
discerned	developed
disproportionate	not equal number

E-F
entitlement	things we are supposed to have
evidence	proof
fascinated	very interested in

G-H
gangly look	long, thin legs and arms
heighten conflicts	increase disagreements
hollow ball	ball which is empty in the middle

I
illustrate	show
inadequate	not enough
indignity	not treated with respect
influential	to have impact
inhibited	not willing to do many things
innate	to be born with
investigate	study
invulnerable	to feel nothing can hurt them

J
joints stiffen   bones are not able to move as well
L
loud wails   to cry loudly
M
magnified   to get bigger
milestones   important points
mittens   similar to gloves for the hands
modified   changed
moody   sometimes get sad and grumpy
mortality   death
N
nondescript word   a word that does not describe
notoriously   well known to be
nourished   feed
O
oblivious   not noticing
orient   get used to
P
perpetuate   keep it going
posed   stated
possessive words   words which show who something belongs to
postpone   to do later
pressing concern   important issue
profound   very important
prosocial behavior   actions that help other people
R
rattle   baby's toy which makes a noise
reared   to grown up in
rent   torn
replied   answered
reproduce   to make again
reserved   quiet
revere   respect
rigidly   firmly; not flexible
rudimentary   basic
runway   pathway
S
sacrificing   giving up
shallow   not deep
siblings   brothers or sisters
skipping   walking and hopping
subtle deception   to fool someone without being obvious
T
timid   shy
turmoil   upset
U
unpopularity   not being liked by other people
V
vanishes   goes away
victimized   to be hurt by others
virtually everything   almost all

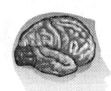

Multiple Choice Posttest

After studying the text and completing the Study Guide activities, answer these questions to determine if you need to review any areas before the course exam.

1. People born during the same period of historical time are called _____.
   a. a cohort
   b. a peerage
   c. a cross-sectional group
   d. a convergent group

2. Concrete operational stage is to _____ as formal operational stages is to _____.
   a. abstract; logical
   b. logical; abstract
   c. conservation; centration
   d. egocentrism; ethnocentrism

3. _____ refers to an individual who perceives everything from his or her own perspective.
   a. Conservation
   b. Ethnocentrism
   c. Egocentrism
   d. Anthropomorphism

4. Focusing on the resulting concrete consequences of a behavior is demonstrated in the _____ level of moral thinking.
   a. concrete operational
   b. preconventional
   c. conventional
   d. postconventional

5. The _____ process teaches children what behaviors and attitudes are appropriate in their family, friends, and culture.
   a. attachment
   b. imprinting
   c. socialization
   d. autonomy

6. Authoritative parents are to _____ children as permissive parents are to _____ children.
   a. distrustful; assertive
   b. passive; assertive
   c. self-reliant; dependent
   d. distrustful; dependent

7. The onset of sexual maturation in adolescence is known as _____.
   a. the growth spurt
   b. maturation
   c. atrophy
   d. puberty

8. Menarche is the _____.
   a. beginning of adolescence
   b. production of sperm cells
   c. onset of menstruation
   d. appearance of pubic hair

9. Due to _____ many adolescents believe that they are invulnerable to danger.
   a. role diffusion
   b. the adolescent delusion
   c. the personal fable
   d. animism

10. What percent of adolescents drop out of high school?
    a. 5-10
    b. 10-15
    c. 15-30
    d. 30-40

11. According to Erikson developing a stable sense of self and making the transition from dependence on others to dependence on oneself is called _____.
    a. self-actualization
    b. identity formation
    c. the personal fable
    d. identity diffusion

12. Rebecca is attending community college to explore various career choices and has put off making a career decision. She BEST fits the description of a(n) _____.
    a. identity achiever
    b. identity diffusion
    c. identity foreclosure
    d. identity moratorium

13. The suicide rate among adolescents has increased by _____ percent since 1950.
    a. 30
    b. 50
    c. 100
    d. 300

14. _____ is an eating disorder that involves eating excessive amount of food followed by purging to get rid of the food.
    a. Hypoglycemia
    b. Anorexia nervosa
    c. Bulimia
    d. Depression

15. According to Erikson, young people are not capable of truly loving someone until they have developed _____.
    a. a sense of identity
    b. compassion
    c. sexual maturity
    d. formal operational thought

16. Most older couples report that the BEST years of their marriage were the years _____.
    a. when they were newlyweds
    b. when their children were young
    c. when their children were teenagers
    d. after their children had grown and left home

17. The majority of older adults are _____.
    a. impotent and incapable of sexual response
    b. uninterested in sex
    c. sexually active
    d. none of the above

18. Kubler-Ross describes the sequence of stages of dying as _____.
    a. anger, denial, depression, bargaining, acceptance
    b. denial, anger, bargaining, depression, acceptance
    c. denial, bargaining, depression, anger, acceptance
    d. anger, bargaining, depression, denial, acceptance

19. Which of the following is NOT a predictor of violent behavior in a young person?
    a. receiving harsh punishment in childhood
    b. a family history of violence
    c. having a history of impulsive and fearless behavior
    d. having Down syndrome

Answers and Explanations to Multiple Choice Posttest

1. a.
2. b.
3. c.
4. b.   A person at the preconventional moral developmental stage focuses on the concrete consequence of their behavior, and not the larger moral issues.
5. c.
6. c.
7. d.
8. c.
9. c.
10. c.
11. b.
12. d.   Going to college or into the military service to explore career possibilities gives people time off before making any final identity decisions.
13. d.
14. c.
15. a.   The love referred to by this question is mature, unselfish love.
16. d.
17. c.
18. b.
19. d.

Key Vocabulary Terms

Cut-out each term and use as study cards. Definition is on the backside of each term.

Developmental psychology	Fetus
Cross-sectional study	Placenta
Cohort	Critical period
Longitudinal study	Neonate
Biographical or retrospective study	Rooting Reflex
Prenatal development	Sucking reflex
Embryo	Swallowing reflex

Developing human between 3 months after conception and birth.	Study of the changes that occur in people from birth through old age.
Organ by which an embryo or fetus is attached to its Mother's uterus and that nourishes it during prenatal developmental.	Method of studying developmental changes by examining groups of subjects who are of different ages.
Time when certain internal and external influences have a major effect on development; at other periods, the same influences will have little or no effect.	Group of people born during the same period in historical time.
Newborn baby.	Method of studying developmental changes by examining the same group of subjects two or more times, as they grow older.
Reflex that causes a newborn to turn its head toward something touching its cheek and to grope around with its mouth.	Method of studying developmental changes by reconstructing subject's past through interviews and investigating the effects of events that occurred in the past on current behaviors.
Reflex that causes that causes the newborn baby to suck on objects placed in its mouth.	Development from conception to birth.
Reflex that enables the newborn baby to swallow liquids without choking.	Developing human between 2 weeks and 3 months after conception.

Grasping reflex	Mental representation
Stepping reflex	Preoperational stage
Temperament	Egocentric
Maturation	Concrete operational stage
Developmental norms	Formal operational stage
Sensory-motor stage	Holophrase
Object permanence	Language acquisition device

Mental image or symbol used to think about or remember an object, a person, or an event.	Reflex that causes newborn babies to close their fists around anything that is put in their hands.
In Piaget's theory, the stage of cognitive development between 2 and 7 years of age, in which the individual becomes able to use mental representations and language to describe, remember, and reason.	Reflex that causes newborn babies to make little stepping motions if they are held upright with their feet just touching a surface.
Unable to see things from another's point of view.	Term used by psychologists to describe the physical/emotional characteristics of the newborn child and young infant; also referred to as personality.
In Piaget's theory, the stage of cognitive development between 7 and 11 years of age, in which the individual can attend to more than one thing at a time and understand someone else's point of view.	Automatic biological unfolding of development in an organism as a function of the passage of time.
In Piaget's theory, the stage of cognitive development between 11 and 15 years of age, in which the individual becomes capable of abstract thought.	Ages by which an average child achieves various developmental milestones.
One-word sentences, commonly used by children under 2 years of age.	In Piaget's theory, the stage of cognitive development between birth and 2 years of age, in which the individual develops object permanence and acquires the ability to form mental representations.
An internal mechanism for processing speech that is "wired into" all humans.	The concept that things continue to exist even when they are out of sight.

Imprinting	Gender identity
Attachment	Gender constancy
Autonomy	Sex-role awareness
Socialization	Sex-typed behavior
Solitary play	Puberty
Parallel play	Menarche
Cooperative play	Imaginary audience

	Form of primitive bonding seen in some species of animals; the newborn animal has a tendency to follow the first moving thing (usually its mother) it sees after it is born or hatched.
A little girl's knowledge that she is a girl, and a little boy's knowledge that he is a boy.	
The realization by a child that gender cannot be changed.	Emotional bond that develops in the first year of life that makes human babies cling to their caregivers for safety and comfort.
Knowledge of what behavior is appropriate for each gender.	Sense of independence; desire not to be controlled by others.
Socially prescribed ways of behaving that differ for boys and girls.	Process by which children learn the behaviors and attitudes appropriate to their family and their culture.
Onset of sexual maturation, with accompanying physical development.	A child engaged in some activity alone; the earliest form of play.
First menstrual period.	Two children playing side by side at the same activities, paying little or no attention to each other; the earliest kind of social interaction between toddlers.
Elkind's term for adolescents; delusion that they are constantly being observed by others.	Two or more children engaged in play that requires interaction.

Personal fable	Midlife crisis
Identity formation	Midlife transition
Identity crisis	Menopause
Peer group	Alzheimer's disease
Clique	
Anorexia nervosa	
Bulimia	

A time when adults discover they no longer feel fulfilled in their jobs or personal lives and attempt to make a decisive shift in career or lifestyle.	Elkind's term for adolescents; delusion that they are unique, very important; and invulnerable.
According to Levinson, a process whereby adults assess the past and formulate new goals for the future.	Erikson's term for the development of a stable sense of self necessity to make the transition from dependence on others to dependence on oneself.
Time in a woman's life when menstruation ceases.	Period of intense self-examination and decision making; part of the process of identity formation.
A disorder common in late adulthood that is characterized by progressive losses in memory and changes in personality . It is believed to be caused by a deterioration of the brain's structure and function.	A network of same-aged friends and acquaintances who give one another emotional and social support.
	Group of adolescents with similar interests and strong mutual attachment.
	A serious eating disorder that is associated with an intense fear of weight gain and a distorted body image.
	An eating disorder characterized by binges of eating followed by self-induced vomiting.

Label Drawings

What does this drawing show?

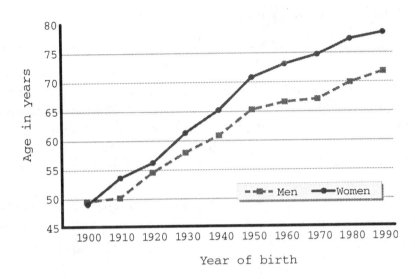

What disorder does this child have and what caused it?

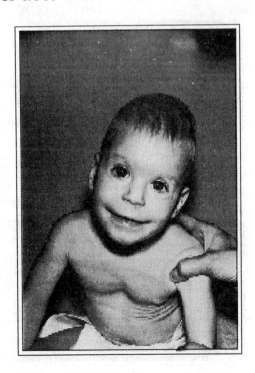

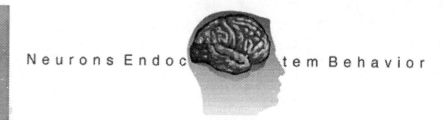

Neurons Endoc... tem Behavior

Overview

· ·

MOTIVATION AND EMOTION

9

Class and Text Notes

This outline provides a way to organize your notes from both the text and the lecture. It will also serve as review sheets for the exam.

Perspectives on Motivation

    Instincts

    Drive

    Drive-Reduction theory

    Homeostasis

    Incentives

Primary Drives

    Hunger

Thirst

Sex

Biological Factors in Sexual Response
Pheromones

Psychological and Cultural Influences

Stimulus Motives

Exploration and Curiosity

Manipulation

Contact

Learned Motives

Aggression

Sexual Coercion and Its Effects

Achievement

Power

Affiliation

A Hierarchy of Motives

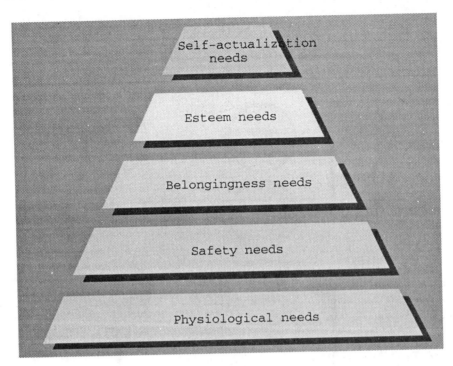

Emotions

Basic Emotional Experiences

Theories of Emotion

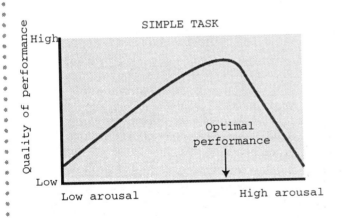

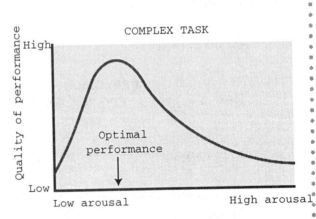

Three Major Theories of Emotions

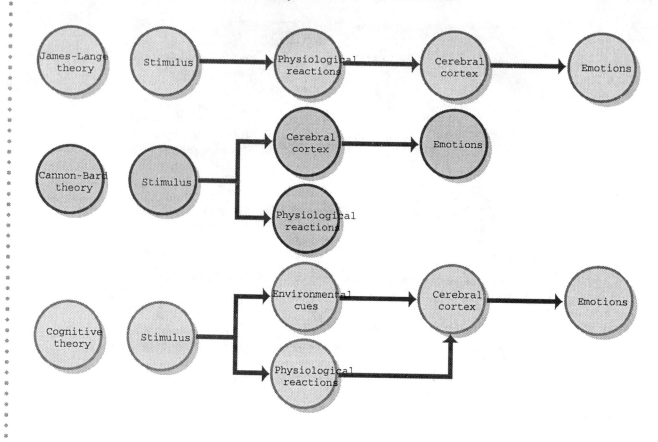

The Expression of Emotion

Verbal Communication

Nonverbal Communication

Gender Differences in Emotion

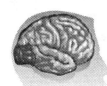

Multiple Choice Pretest

This pretest will help you identify the topics in the chapter that are most difficult for you. By focusing your study time in those areas, you will see the greatest improvement.

1. A(n) _____ is a need that pushes a person to work toward a specific goal.
   a. stimulus
   b. incentive
   c. behavior
   d. motive

2. A(n) _____ is an inborn, goal-directed behavior that is seen in an entire species.
   a. instinct
   b. motive
   c. drive
   d. stimulus

3. Our bodies try to maintain _____, which is a state of balance.
   a. acquiescence
   b. incentives
   c. homeostasis
   d. reciprocity

4. External stimuli that lead to goal-directed behavior are called _____.
   a. drives
   b. needs
   c. incentives
   d. reciprocals

5. All of the following are examples of primary drives EXCEPT
   a. hunger
   b. thirst
   c. money
   d. affiliation

6. Our body regulates metabolism, fat storage, and food intake to maintain a specific weight. This homeostatic mechanism is called
   _____.
   a. a reciprocal feedback center
   b. set point
   c. the drive reduction center
   d. the satiety center

7. Increased _____ is the most effective way to increase the body's metabolism when trying to lose weight.
   a. protein consumption
   b. reduction of calories
   c. exercise
   d. sleep

8. Lower testosterone levels result in decreased sexual desire in _____.
   a. men only
   b. women only
   c. both men and women
   d. neither men nor women

9. Scents that can be sexually stimulating are called _____.
   a. androgens
   b. corticorsteroids
   c. globulins
   d. pheromones

10. Hiking in a cave could satisfy each of the following EXCEPT _____.
    a. exploration motive
    b. activity motive
    c. curiosity motive
    d. contact motive

11. Purposefully inflicting harm on others is known as _____ behavior.
    a. anger-driven
    b. violent
    c. aggressive
    d. confrontational

12. About _____ wives are physically abused in the United States each year.
    a. 150,000
    b. 350,000
    c. 550,00
    d. 750,000

13. The emotion of _____ is most closely related to aggression.
    a. depression
    b. pain
    c. frustration
    d. conflict

14. Most psychologists believe that aggression is _____.
    a. an innate biological response to frustration
    b. linked to sexual drive
    c. a learned response
    d. a drive that builds up over time and must be released

15. In about two-thirds of rapes, the most important motive was _____.
    a. attraction
    b. power
    c. sexual satisfaction
    d. sadism

16. The _____ motive is related to the need to influence or control other people.
    a. social
    b. achievement
    c. status
    d. power

17. A need to be with other people is called a(n) _____ need.
    a. social
    b. affiliation
    c. status
    d. power

18. The highest level of motive according to Maslow is _____.
    a. physiological need
    b. self-actualization
    c. esteem needs
    d. need for success

19. Chronically _____ 40-year-olds had elevated levels of a harmful form of cholesterol.
    a. angry
    b. depressed
    c. worried
    d. anxious

Answers and Explanations to Multiple Choice Pretest

1. d.
2. a.
3. c.
4. c.
5. c. Primary needs are basic needs we are born with; such as, hunger, thirst, sexual drive, and comfort.
6. b.
7. c. Exercise is the best way to prevent metabolism from dropping when dieting.
8. c. Men and women both produce testosterone. Women just produce less of it.
9. d.
10. d. Contact motives refers to touch.
11. c. Aggression is any action that hurts someone. This can be verbal and not always considered violent.
12. b.
13. c.
14. c.
15. b.
16. d.
17. b.
18. b.
19. a. Anger has a detrimental effect on a person's body.

Learning Objectives

After you have read and studied this chapter, you should be able to complete the following statements. Your exam is written based on these learning objectives.

1. Define motive and emotion and explain the roles of stimulus, behavior, and goals in motivation.

2. Identify the primary drives and their physiological bases.

3. Describe how hunger is controlled in the brain. Explain how external cues and experience influence hunger.

4. Explain how the thirst regulators in the body work.

5. List the biological factors involved in the sex drive. Discuss psychological influences on sexual motivation. List the causes of sexual dysfunction.

6. List the characteristics of the following stimulus motives: activity, exploration, curiosity, manipulation, and contact.

7. Define aggression. Discuss three theories of aggressive behavior.

8. Explain why the need for achievement is so strong in some people.

9. Define sexual coercion and explain its effects.

10. Distinguish between the motives for power and achievement. Give an example.

11. Explain how the affiliation motives are aroused.

12. Identify the five categories in Maslow's hierarchy of motives.

13. Describe and give an example of each of the three basic categories of emotions.

14. Summarize the Yerkes-Dodson law.

15. Explain how Plutchik categorized emotions.

16. Describe and differentiate among the James-Lange, Cannon-Bard, cognitive, and Izard's theories of emotion.

17. List three reasons why people may not be able or willing to report their emotions.

18. Identify several kinds of nonverbal communications. Give one example of each kind.

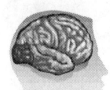

Short Essay Questions

Write out your answers to the following four essay questions to further your mastery of the topics.

1. Explain drive reduction theory and how it relates to the concept of homeostasis.

_____

_____

_____

_____

_____

_____

_____

_____

_____

_____

2. Discuss the most effective methods for losing weight and maintaining the weight loss.

_____

_____

_____

_____

_____

_____

_____

_____

3. Explain the Yerkes-Dodson law and how its principles affect everyday functioning.

_____

_____

_____

_____

_____

_____

_____

_____

_____

_____

4. Discuss gender differences in the experience and expression of emotion.

_____

_____

_____

_____

_____

_____

_____

_____

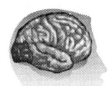

Language Support

Students identified the following words from the text as needing more explanation. This page can be cut-out, folded in half, and used as a bookmark for this chapter.

A
accomplices	working with them
affiliation	connect with other people
agile	capable of fine movement
ambiguous	not clear
annoyed	upset
anxious	not calm
appealing	looks good

B
battered women	women who are hit and hurt by a family member
betrayed	dishonored
bristled	stood up
bumpy flight	airplane that moves suddenly in several directions

C
chronically	continually
cling	hold on to
coherent	organized and makes sense
contradictory	two opposites at the same time
convert	change
coupled	together with
criticized	bad things being said about a person

D
degraded	put down with words
deliberately	on purpose
dense	tightly packed together
deter	stop
diffuse	spread out
discourage	make them want to give up
distinct	different; separate
domesticated animals	animals that are comfortable living with people

E
eliciting	getting
embrace	hug
entail	involve
extracellular	outside of the cell

F
fantasies	stories in the mind
frowning	a sad facial expression

G
gory	showing horrible, bloody things
growling dog	a dog which is making a low sound to show it is angry

H
hatred	to hate
hypothetical situations	made up stories or examples

I

implicitly	by nature
impostors	people that are acting like something they are not
in the midst of	in the middle of
inaccurate	not right
infallible	never wrong
innate	born with
insignificant	not important
instantaneous	very fast
instincts	knowledge people are born with

L

less spectacular	not important

M

manipulating	to handle with our hands
massaged	rubbed
mere	just; only
milkshake	a drink made out of milk and sugar
mimic	look or act like

N

notion	idea

O

obtained	found
oversupply	too many

P

parlor	room for entertaining friends
pickpocket	someone who steals from people's pockets and purses
portrayed	shown
predecessors	those that came before
presumed	believed
prevalent	common

R

replenish	to fill up again

S

sadism	enjoy hurting others
satiety	feeling full
says acidly	said with anger
self-preservation	to take care of oneself
sexual harassment	to feel threatened by someone's sexual words or behavior
slamming	throwing down hard
smell wafting	smell drifting out of

T

terrycloth	material towels are made out of
thunderstorm	bad weather that includes light flashes and loud noises
triggered	started

V

vigorous	high energy

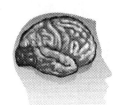

Multiple Choice Posttest

After studying the text and completing the Study Guide activities, answer these questions to determine if you need to review any areas before the course exam.

1. We are moved toward some _____ by both motives and emotions.
   a. stimulus
   b. homeostasis
   c. action
   d. equilibrium

2. Hunger or thirst are examples of a state of tension and these are called _____.
   a. drives
   b. homeostasis
   c. impulse
   d. instinct

3. Biking at the beach could satisfy each of the following EXCEPT _____.
   a. exploration motive
   b. activity motive
   c. curiosity motive
   d. contact motive

4. A difference in animal and human sex drives is that _____.
   a. human sex drive is controlled by the male's reproductive system
   b. humans are able to be interested in sex at any time
   c. human sex drive is controlled by hormones
   d. human sex drive is controlled by the females' reproductive system

5. Men tend to be more sexually aroused by _____.
   a. visual cues
   b. auditory cues
   c. olfactory cues
   d. touch

6. Women tend to be more sexually aroused by _____.
   a. visual cues
   b. auditory cues
   c. olfactory cues
   d. touch

7. Most psychologists believe that aggression is _____.
   a. an innate biological response to frustration
   b. linked to sexual drive
   c. a learned response
   d. a drive that builds up over time and must be released

8. According to Chodorow, the differences in male/female sexuality result from _____.
   a. different expectations and standards of treatment from parents, particularly fathers
   b. the different developmental tasks facing boys and girls as they separate from their female caregiver.
   c. an evolutionary perspective where is advantageous for males to impregnate as many women as possible, but is advantageous for women to be selective about how many males they have sex with
   d. different social and cultural cues such a society's double standard for men and women

9. A need to be with other people is called a(n) _____ need.
   a. social
   b. affiliation
   c. status
   d. power

10. The most basic level of motive according to Maslow is _____.
    a. physiological need
    b. self-actualization
    c. esteem needs
    d. need for success

11. In Harlow's classic experiments, when the infant monkeys were frightened they ran to a surrogate "mother" that offered _____.
    a. food and warmth
    b. food only
    c. warmth only
    d. warmth and closeness

12. According to research done by the FBI,
    _____ percent of married couples had en-
    gaged in physical violence in their married
    lives.
    a. 25
    b. 35
    c. 45
    d. 55

13. Bandura describes the relationship between
    frustration and aggression as which of the
    following?
    a. Unintentional interference with a task will
       lead people to become more aggressive.
    b. Frustration generates aggression only in
       those people who have learned aggression
       as a coping mechanism.
    c. Frustration almost always leads to
       aggression.
    d. Frustration is the least important among
       several types of experiences that can
       provoke aggression.

14. Women who have been forced to have sex
    frequently experience the symptoms of
    _____.
    a. generalized anxiety disorder
    b. bipolar disorder
    c. post-traumatic stress disorder
    d. obsessive-compulsive disorder

15. Which of the following is likely to be signifi-
    cantly affected by emotional level according to
    the Yerkes-Dodson law?
    a. watching T.V.
    b. gardening
    c. taking the college board exams
    d. taking notes in an introductory psychology
       class

16. The theory which maintain that emotions are
    caused by the interaction of physiological
    processes and perception of the situation is the
    _____ theory.
    a. James-Lange
    b. activation theory
    c. Cannon-Bard theory
    d. cognitive theory

Answers and Explanations to Multiple Choice Posttest

1. c. Both motives and emotions motivate us to
      take action.

2. a.

3. d.

4. b.

5. a.

6. d.

7. c.

8. b.

9. b.

10. a.

11. d.

12. a.

13. b.

14. c.

15. c. Yerkes-Dodson Law states that the more
       complex the task, the lower the level of
       arousal that can be tolerated before perfor-
       mance deteriorates.

16. d.

Key Vocabulary Terms

Cut-out each term and use as study cards.
Definition is on the backside of each term.

Motive	Primary drive
Emotion	Set point
Instinct	Testosterone
Drive	Pheromones
Drive-reduction theory	Stimulus motive
Homeostasis	Social motive
Incentive	Aggression

Physiologically based unlearned motive (e.g., hunger).	Specific need, desire, or want, such as hunger, thirst, or achievement, that energizes and directs goal-oriented behavior.
A homeostatic mechanism in the body that regulates metabolism, fat storage, and food intake so as to maintain a preprogrammed weight.	Feeling, such as fear, joy, or surprise, that energizes and directs behavior.
Hormone that is the primary determinant of the sex drive in both men and women.	Inborn, inflexible, goal-directed behavior that is characteristic of an entire species.
Substances secreted by some animals; when scented, they enhance the sexual readiness of the other sex.	State of tension or arousal due to biological needs.
Unlearned motive, such as curiosity or activity, that pushes us to explore or change the world around us.	Theory that motivated behavior is directed toward reducing a state of bodily tension or arousal and returning the organism to homeostasis.
Learned motive associated with relationships among people, such as the needs for affiliation, achievement, and power.	State of balance and stability in which the organism functions effectively.
Behavior aimed at doing harm to others; also the motive to behave aggressively.	External stimulus that prompts goal-directed behavior.

Achievement motive	
Power motive	
Affiliation motive	
Yerkes-Dodson law	
James-Lange theory	
Cannon-Bard theory	
Cognitive theory	

	The need to excel, to overcome obstacles; a social motive.
	The need to win recognition or to influence or control other people or groups; a social motive.
	The need to be with others; a social motive.
	States that there is an optimal level of arousal for the best performance of any task; the more complex the task, the lower the level of arousal that can be tolerated before performance deteriorates.
	States that stimuli cause physiological changes in our bodies, and emotions result from those physiological changes.
	States that the experience of emotion occurs simultaneously with biological changes.
	States that emotional experiences depends on one's perception or judgment of the situation one is in.

Label Drawings

Fill-In the Blanks

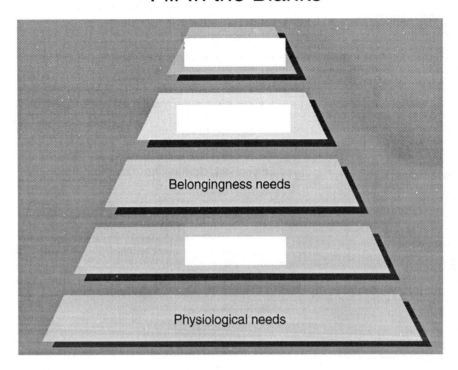

Belongingness needs

Physiological needs

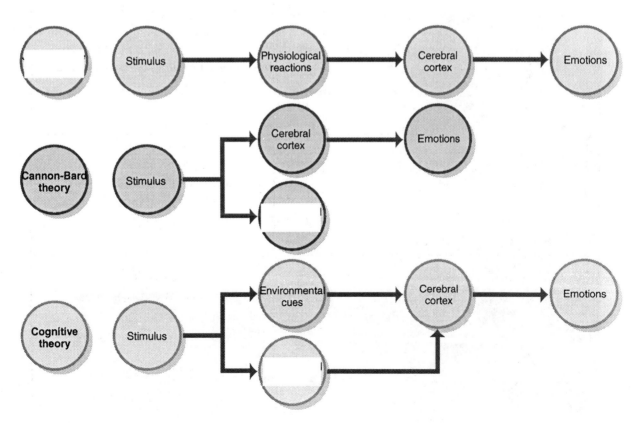

Stimulus → Physiological reactions → Cerebral cortex → Emotions

Cannon-Bard theory — Stimulus → Cerebral cortex → Emotions

Cognitive theory — Stimulus → Environmental cues → Cerebral cortex → Emotions

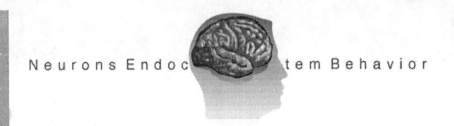

Overview

• •

PERSONALITY

10

Class and Text Notes

This outline provides a way to organize your notes from both the text and the lecture. It will also serve as review sheets for the exam.

The Case of Jaylene Smith

Psychodynamic Theories

Sigmund Freud

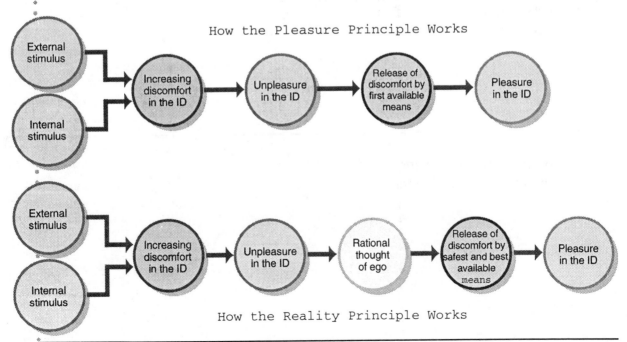

How the Pleasure Principle Works

External stimulus
Internal stimulus
→ Increasing discomfort in the ID → Unpleasure in the ID → Release of discomfort by first available means → Pleasure in the ID

External stimulus
Internal stimulus
→ Increasing discomfort in the ID → Unpleasure in the ID → Rational thought of ego → Release of discomfort by safest and best available means → Pleasure in the ID

How the Reality Principle Works

Theories of Personality

Theory	Roots of Personality	Methods of Assessing
Psychodynamic	Unconscious thoughts, feelings, motives, and conflicts; repressed problems from early childhood.	Projective tests, personal interivews.
Humanistic	A drive toward personal growth and higher levels of functioning.	Objective tests and personal interviews.
Trait	Relatively permanent dispositions within the individual that cause the person to think, feel, and act in characteristic ways.	Objective tests.
Social Learning Theories	Determined by past reinforcement and punishment as well as by observing what happens to other people.	Interviews, objective tests, observations.

The Consistency Controversy

Cognitive-Social Learning Theories

A Cognitive-Social Learning View of Jaylene Smith
Evaluating Cognitive-Social Learning Theories

Personality Assessment

The Personal Interview

Observation

Objective Tests

Projective Tests

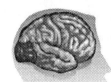

Multiple Choice Pretest

This pretest will help you identify the topics in the chapter that are most difficult for you. By focusing your study time in those areas, you will see the greatest improvement.

1. _____ is defined as the characteristic pattern of thoughts, feelings, and behavior that is stable over time and distinguishes one person from another.
   a. Learning
   b. Personality
   c. Habit
   d. Trait

2. Personality is shaped by a motive for personal growth and reaching one's maximum potential, according to _____ theories.
   a. psychodynamic
   b. trait
   c. humanistic
   d. social-cognitive

3. Personality is the result of unconscious, often sexual, motivations and conflicts, according to _____ theories.
   a. psychodynamic
   b. trait
   c. humanistic
   d. social-cognitive

4. Personality is shaped by the ways people think about, act on and respond to their environment, according to _____ theories.
   a. psychodynamic
   b. trait
   c. humanistic
   d. social-cognitive

5. The term "sexual instinct", according to Freud, refers to _____.
   a. childhood experience
   b. desire for any pleasure
   c. erotic sexuality
   d. personal unconscious

6. According to Freud, the unconscious urges seek expression through the _____.
   a. id   b. ego
   c. superego   d. persona

7. Which of the following is MOST likely to be true regarding Jaylene Smith, in the case study presented in your text?
   a. Her personality is the result of an unresolved Oedipal complex and fixation in the phallic stage of development.
   b. Her personality is the result of certain inborn traits such as determination and persistence.
   c. Her personality is a reflection of a complex interaction of inherited predispositions, life experiences, and learned behaviors
   d. Her personality is a reflection of a discrepancy between her self-concept and her inborn capacities.

8. According to Freud, the reality principle is _____.
   a. the way in which the ego tries to delay satisfying the id's desires until it can do so safely and successfully
   b. the way in which the id tries to obtain immediate gratification and avoid pain
   c. the way in which the ego ideal established standards of what one would like to be
   d. the way in which young children instinctively seek self-actualization

9. The standard of perfection by which the superego judges the ego's actions is known as the _____, in Freud theory.
   a. ego-ideal
   b. conscience
   c. animus
   d. archetype

10. When our superego is dominant, _____.
    a. we are able to fully enjoy a normal life
    b. we do not have any guilt feelings
    c. our drives are not regulated
    d. our behavior is too tightly controlled

11. Jim is impulsive and emotional. His behavior is illogical and he feels little guilt for what he does. Freud would say John's _____ is the dominant part of his personality.
    a. id
    b. ego
    c. superego
    d. persona

12. Freud calls the energy generated by the sexual instinct the _____.
    a. pleasure principle
    b. libido
    c. abreaction
    d. reality principle

13. Freud would have viewed someone who is argumentative, hostile, and lacks self-confidence as probably fixated in the _____ stage.
    a. oral
    b. anal
    c. phallic
    d. genital

14. Jung's theory of personality describes a "mask" which people project as their public self. This mask is known as _____.
    a. anima
    b. ego
    c. shadow
    d. persona

15. Jung called the feminine side of the male personality the _____.
    a. anima
    b. ego
    c. shadow
    d. persona

16. Adler felt that a driving force in shaping personality was overcoming feelings of _____.
    a. basic anxiety
    b. inhibition
    c. inferiority
    d. individualism

17. Ruth is 80 years old. According to Erikson, her main task will be to develop a sense of _____.
    a. trust
    b. intimacy
    c. generativity
    d. integrity

Answers and Explanations to Multiple Choice Pretest

1. b.
2. c.
3. a.
4. d.
5. b.
6. a.
7. c. The case study in the text about Jaylene details a very complex combination of genetic and environmental factors in forming her personality
8. a.
9. a.
10. d. The superego is overly controlled which would result in a person not satisfying enough basic urges.
11. a.
12. b.
13. a.
14. d.
15. a. The anima is the female side of the male personality, and the animus is the male side of the female personality.
16. c.
17. d. Erikson theorized that the developmental task of the elderly is to make sense of their lives. He called this integrity.

Learning Objectives

After you have read and studied this chapter, you should be able to complete the following statements. Your exam is written based on these learning objectives.

1. Define personality.

2. Summarize the interaction of Freud's id, ego, and super-ego.

3. Identify Freud's five stages of psychosexual development.

4. Differentiate between the theories of Jung, Adler, and Horney.

5. Identify Erik Erikson's eight stages of personality development.

6. Explain object relations theories of personality.

7. Contrast Carl Rogers' humanistic theory with Freudian theory.

8. Explain trait theory.

9. Explain Mischel's situationism and the concept of interactionism.

10. Compare cognitive social-learning theories to early views of personality.

11. Describe the four basic tools psychologists use to measure personality.

12. List two objective tests to their uses. List the advantages and disadvantages of objective test.

13. Discuss the advantages of projective tests. Explain how the Rorschach Test and the Thematic Apperception Test are administered.

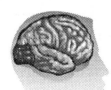

Short Essay Questions

Write out your answers to the following eight essay questions to further your mastery of the topics.

1. Explain how each of the four major types of personality theories views personality.

_____

_____

_____

_____

_____

_____

_____

_____

_____

_____

_____

2. Describe the function of each part of Freud's structure of personality.

_____

_____

_____

_____

_____

_____

_____

_____

_____

3. Describe Horney's theory of personality and contrast it to Freud's personality theory.

_____

_____

_____

_____

_____

_____

_____

_____

_____

_____

_____

4. Identify Freud's psychosexual stages, when they occur, and the effects of problems occurring at each stage.

_____

_____

_____

_____

_____

_____

_____

_____

_____

5. Describe the role of archetypes in Carl Jung's personality theory.

_____

_____

_____

_____

_____

_____

_____

_____

_____

_____

_____

6. Identify what Adler felt were the driving forces of personality and how his views changed over time.

_____

_____

_____

_____

_____

_____

_____

_____

_____

7. List the stages of Erikson's theory of development in chronological order, and briefly explain the associated conflict

_____

_____

_____

_____

_____

_____

_____

_____

_____

_____

_____

8. Compare and contrast the strengths and weaknesses of various measures of personality: the interview, observation, objective tests, and projective tests.

_____

_____

_____

_____

_____

_____

_____

_____

_____

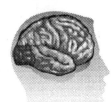

Language Support

Students identified the following words from the text as needing more explanation. This page can be cut-out, folded in half, and used as a bookmark for this chapter.

A
altercation — disagreement
ambiguous — not clear
amiable — friendly
attain — reach

B
bickering — fighting

C
capture — include
coherent — logical and organized
conditional — depend on
conquering — winning
consensus — number of people who agree
continuity — being continuous
cordial — polite

D
descriptors — something which explains a quality
disheartening — sad and discouraging
disposition — personality
drawbacks — problems

E
elicit — bring out
embodied — part of
evident — able to be seen

F
fate — what happens in a person's life
fosters — leads to

H
hallmark of maturity — important sign of maturity
hostility — anger

I
infer — conclude; reason
instances — times
intensified — got stronger
intuiting — to understand through getting a feeling about something

L
lofty — very high

M
maintain — keep
marine sergeant — a military officer in the marine corp.
mediocre — poor quality
millennia — 1,000 years
misinterpret — get a wrong understanding of something
mysticism — spiritual approach focused on gaining direct communication with God

N
narcissism   to love oneself too much
nonessential   not necessary
O
one-dimensional   only one part
P
pessimistic   look at things in a negative (bad) way
pursue   go after
R
recruits   low ranking soldiers
retaining   keeping in
rivalry   competition
S
salient   important
self-restraint   control of oneself
shifted the focus   changed the main concern
T
thrived   grew very well
U
unique   unusual

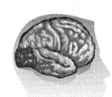

Multiple Choice Posttest

After studying the text and completing the Study Guide activities, answer these questions to determine if you need to review any areas before the course exam.

1. Which of the following is NOT an aspect of personality?
   a. enduring
   b. unique
   c. stable
   d. unpredictable

2. _____ theories state that personality is shaped by a motive for personal growth and reaching one's maximum potential.
   a. Psychodynamic
   b. Trait
   c. Humanistic
   d. Social-cognitive

3. According to _____ theories, personality is the result of unconscious, often sexual, motivations and conflicts.
   a. psychodynamic
   b. trait
   c. humanistic
   d. social-cognitive

4. According to Freud, the unconscious urges seek expression through the _____.
   a. id
   b. ego
   c. superego
   d. persona

5. When our id is dominant, _____.
   a. we are able to fully enjoy a normal life
   b. we do not have any guilt feelings
   c. our drives are not regulated
   d. our behavior is too tightly controlled

6. Jung called the male side of the female personality the _____.
   a. anima
   b. animus
   c. shadow
   d. persona

7. Adler felt that a driving force in shaping personality was overcoming feelings of

   _____.
   a. basic anxiety
   b. inhibition
   c. inferiority
   d. individualism

8. In the Jaylene Smith case study in the text, Erikson's theory would see the root of her problem as her inability to establish a sense of

   _____.
   a. trust
   b. generativity
   c. autonomy
   d. identity

9. Carl Rogers theorized that people brought up with unconditional positive regard

   _____.
   a. are unlikely to be fully functioning
   b. tend to be vain and narcissistic
   c. live lives directed toward what others want and value
   d. feel valued

10. It appears that people tend to learn to perceive events in their lives optimistically or pessimistically _____.
    a. at an early age
    b. during college
    c. during young adulthood
    d. during middle age

11. A person's expectancies become a critical part of his or her _____, according to Bandura and Rotter.
    a. self-actualization
    b. explanatory style
    c. ideal self
    d. persona

12. When explaining personality, cognitive-social learning theorists put _____ at the center of personality.
    a. unconscious processes
    b. emotional stability
    c. mental processes
    d. environmental cues

13. The most widely used objective personality test is the _____.
    a. 16PF
    b. TAT
    c. Rorschach
    d. MMPI

14. A behaviorist would prefer _____ when assessing someone's personality.
    a. objective tests
    b. observation
    c. interviews
    d. projective tests

15. Psychodynamic theorists believe that objective tests are of little use because _____.
    a. they are usually not valid
    b. it is difficult to agree on the meaning of test results
    c. they are difficult to score
    d. people are not usually aware of the unconscious determinants of their behavior

16. The Rorschach test relies on the interpretation of _____ to understand personality.
    a. 16 part questionnaire
    b. cards with human figures on them
    c. 10 cards containing ink blots
    d. sentence completion exercises

17. The male gender identity is largely established through a process of _____, according to Chodorow.
    a. compensation
    b. attachment
    c. reinforcement
    d. individuation

Answers to Multiple Choice Posttest

1. d.
2. c.
3. a.
4. a.
5. c.
6. b.
7. c.
8. a.
9. d.
10. a.
11. b.
12. c.
13. d.
14. b.
15. d.
16. c.
17. d.

Key Vocabulary Terms
Cut-out each term and use as study cards.
Definition is on the backside of each term.

Personality	Reality principle
Psychodynamic theories	Superego
Unconscious	Ego ideal
Psychoanalysis	Libido
Id	Fixation
Pleasure principle	Oral stage
Ego	Anal stage

According to Freud, the way in which the ego seeks to satisfy instinctual demands safely and effectively in the real world.	An individual's unique pattern of thoughts, feelings, and behaviors that persist over time and across situations.
According to Freud, the social and parental standards the individual has internalized; the conscience and the ego ideal.	Personality theories that consider behavior to result from psychological dynamics that go on within the individual, often beyond conscious awareness.
The part of the superego that consists of standards of what one would like to be.	In Freud's theory, all the ideas, thoughts, and feelings of which we are not and normally cannot become aware.
According to Freud, the energy generated by the sexual instinct.	The theory of personality Freud developed as well as the form of therapy he invented.
According to Freud, a partial or complete halt at some point in the individual's psychosexual development.	In Freud's theory of personality, the collection of unconscious urges and desires that continually seek expression.
First stage in Freud's theory of personality development in which the infant's erotic feelings center on the mouth, lips, and tongue.	According to Freud, the way in which the id seeks immediate gratification of an instinct.
Second stage in Freud's theory of personality development, in which a child's erotic feelings center on the anus and on elimination.	According to Freud, the art of the personality that mediates between environmental demands (reality), conscience (superego), and instinctual needs (id); now often used as a synonym for "self."

Phallic stage	Persona
Oedipus and Electra complex	Anima
Latency period	Animus
Genital stage	Extrovert
Personal unconscious	Introvert
Collective unconscious	Rational individuals
Archetypes	Irrational individuals

According to Jung, our public self, the mask we put on to represent ourselves to others.	Third stage in Freud's theory of personality development, in which erotic feelings center on the genitals.
According to Jung, the female archetype as it is expressed in their male personality.	According to Freud, a child's sexual attachment to the parent of the opposite sex and jealousy toward the parent of the same sex.
According to Jung, the male archetype as it is expressed in the female personality.	In Freud's theory of personality, a period in which the child appears to have no interest in the opposite sex; occurs after the phallic stage.
According to Jung, a person who usually focuses on social life and the external world instead of on his or her internal experience.	In Freud's theory of personality development, the final stage of normal adult sexual development, which is usually marked by mature sexuality.
According to Jung, a person who usually focuses on his or her own thoughts and feelings.	In Jung's theory of personality, one of the two levels of the unconscious; it contains the individual's repressed thoughts, experiences, and undeveloped ideas.
According to Jung, people who regulate their actions by the psychological functions of thinking and feeling.	In Jung's theory of personality, the level of the unconscious that is inherited and common to all members of a species.
According to Jung, people who base their actions on perceptions, either through the senses (sensation) or through unconscious processes (intuition).	In Jung's theory of personality, thought forms common to human beings, stored in the collective unconscious.

Compensation	Self-actualizing tendency
Inferiority complex	Fully functioning person
Anxiety	Unconditional positive regard
Neurotic trends	Conditional positive regard
Object relations theories	Personality traits
Humanistic personality theory	Factor analysis
Actualizing tendency	Cognitive-social learning theories

According to Rogers, the drive of human beings to fulfill their self-concepts, or the images they have formed of themselves.	According to Adler, the person's effort to effect or overcome imagined or real personal weaknesses.
According to Rogers, an individual whose self-concept closely resembles his or her inborn capacities or potentials.	In Adler's theory, the fixation on feelings of inferiority that results in emotional and social paralysis.
In Rogers' theory, the full acceptance and love of another person regardless of that person's behavior.	In Horney's theory, the individual's reaction to real or imagined threats.
In Rogers' theory, acceptance and love that are predicted on behaving in certain ways and fulfilling certain conditions.	In Horney's theory, irrational strategies for coping with emotional problems and minimizing anxiety.
Dimensions or characteristics on which people differ in distinctive ways.	Psychodynamic theories of personality that emphasize early relations with caregivers as the chief determinant of personality and the basis for subsequent interpersonal relations.
A statistical technique that identifies groups of related objects; used by Cattell to identify trait clusters.	Any personality theory that asserts the fundamental goodness of people and their striving toward higher levels of functioning.
Personality theories that view behavior as the product of the interaction of cognition, learning and past experiences, and the immediate environment.	According to Rogers, the drive of every organism to fulfill its biological potential and to become what it is inherently capable of becoming.

Expectancies	16 Personality Factor Question.
Locus of control	MMPI
Self-efficacy	Projective tests
Performance standards	Rorschach test Thematic
Reciprocal determinism	Apperception Test
Person variables	
Objective tests	

A 374-question objective personality test created by Cattell that provides scores on the 16 traits he identified.	In Bandura's view, what a person anticipates in a situation or as a result of behaving in certain ways.
The most widely used objective personality test, originally intended for psychiatric diagnosis.	According to Rotter, an expectancy about whether reinforcement is under internal or external control.
Personality tests, such as the Rorschach inkblot test; consisting of ambiguous or unstructured material that do not limit the response to be given.	According to Bandura, the expectancy that one's efforts will be successful.
A projective test composed of ambiguous inkblots, the way a person interprets the blots is thought to reveal aspects of his or her personality.	In Bandura's theory, standards that people develop to rate the adequacy of their own behavior in a variety of situations.
A projective test composed of ambiguous pictures about which a person writes stories.	In Bandura's personality model, the concept that the person influences the environment and is in turn influenced by the environment.
	According to Mischel, cognitive processes that influence behavior in different situations.
	Personality tests that are administered and scored in a standard way.

Label Drawings

Fill-In the Blanks

How the Pleasure Principle Works

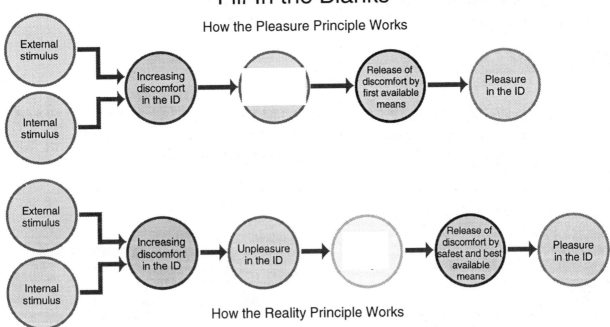

How the Reality Principle Works

Fill-In Roots of Personality

SUMMARY TABLE

Theories of Personality

Theory	Roots of Personality	Methods of Assessing
Psychodynamic		Projective tests, personal interivews.
Humanistic		Objective tests and personal interviews.
Trait		Objective tests.
Social Learning Theories		Interviews, objective tests, observations.

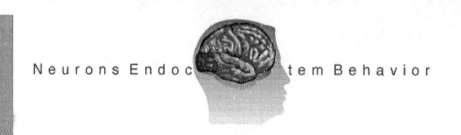

Overview

● ●

STRESS AND HEALTH PSYCHOLOGY

11

....

Class and Text Notes

This outline provides a way to organize your notes from both the text and the lecture. It will also serve as review sheets for the exam.

Sources of Stress

    Change

    Hassles

    Pressure

    Frustration

    Conflict

How Stress Affects Health

Stress and Heart Disease

Stress and the Immune System

Sources of Extreme Stress

1. Unemployment

2. Divorce and separation

3. Bereavement

4. Natural and man-made catastrophes

5. Combat and other threatening personal attacks

The Well-Adjusted Person

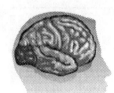

Multiple Choice Pretest

This pretest will help you identify the topics in the chapter that are most difficult for you. By focusing your study time in those areas, you will see the greatest improvement.

1. _____ psychology is a subfield concerned with the relationship between psychological factors and physical health or illness.
   a. Forensic
   b. Neuroimmunology
   c. Environmental
   d. Health

2. A demand that leads to a state of tension or threat and requires change is called _____.
   a. pressure
   b. stress
   c. adjustment
   d. arousal

3. The Social Readjustment Rating Scale measures _____.
   a. the degree to which one has resolved stress
   b. family situations
   c. the degree to which flexibility is genetically determined
   d. how much stress a person has undergone in a given period

4. You are having a difficult time deciding whether to vacation in Hawaii or Tahiti. This type of conflict is called _____.
   a. avoidance/avoidance
   b. approach/approach
   c. avoidance/approach
   d. approach/avoidance

5. Albert Ellis described an internal source of stress due to _____.
   a. hardiness traits
   b. faulty response cues
   c. faulty expectations
   d. irrational beliefs

6. An effective way of coping with a conflict is to _____.
   a. deny the conflict   c. be aggressive
   b. withdraw   d. compromise

7. Freud believed that people use self-deceptive techniques for reducing stress that are called _____.
   a. avoidance behavior
   b. regressive syndrome
   c. maladaptive behavior
   d. defense mechanisms

8. When you forget the embarrassing thing you said at work, you are probably using the defense mechanism of _____.
   a. projection
   b. repression
   c. intellectualization
   d. reaction formation

9. You have to cancel a date with someone and when you do the person starts yelling and calls you names. That person is exhibiting _____.
   a. repression
   b. regression
   c. reaction formation
   d. sublimation

10. Changing a repressed drive into something more socially acceptable is called _____.
    a. repression
    b. regression
    c. reaction formation
    d. sublimation

11. Utilizing a defense mechanism becomes maladaptive when _____.
    a. it leads to superstitious behavior
    b. it protects feelings of self-worth
    c. it interferes with a person's ability to function
    d. people use it a lot

12. Selye describes the General Adaptation Syndrome as proceeding in the following order:
    a. resistance, alarm reaction, exhaustion
    b. alarm reaction, resistance, exhaustion
    c. exhaustion, resistance, alarm reaction
    d. resistance, alarm reaction, exhaustion

13. People who respond to life events in a relaxed and easy going way are exhibiting a _____ behavior pattern.
    a. Type A
    b. Type B
    c. Type E
    d. Type S

14. Which of the following correctly lists the order of reaction to catastrophes?
    a. confusion, rage, recovery
    b. rage, confusion, recovery
    c. suggestible stage, shock stage, recovery stage
    d. shock stage, suggestible stage, recovery stage

15. For someone to heal from posttraumatic disorder depends a great deal on
    _____.
    a. how much emotional support the victim gets from family, friends, and community
    b. whether the person experienced the stressful event alone, or with others
    c. whether the victim is a male or a female
    d. whether the person has an internal or external locus of control

16. Maslow's theory states that individuals who are well-adjusted attempt to
    _____.
    a. remain aloof from the rest of society
    b. convince others that they have no faults
    c. actualize themselves
    d. win others to their way of thinking

17. Research done by Taylor found that mentally healthy people _____ their ability to control chance events and believe that the future will be _____ than the present.
    a. underestimate; worse
    b. accurately estimate; the same
    c. overestimate; better
    d. overestimate; worse

Answers and Explanations to Multiple Choice Pretest

1. d.
2. b.
3. d.
4. b. Deciding between two good alternatives is called an approach/approach conflict.
5. d.
6. d.
7. d.
8. b. Repression is forgetting something that makes us anxious.
9. b.
10. d. Sublimation
11. c. Defense mechanism help us deal with anxiety but they can interfere with normal functioning.
12. b.
13. b.
14. d.
15. a. Support from family, friends, and community is important to someone trying to heal from PTSD.
16. c.
17. c.

Learning Objectives

After you have read and studied this chapter, you should be able to complete the following statements. Your exam is written based on these learning objectives.

1. Define adjustment and stress. Identify sources of stress.

2. Describe the nature of pressure, frustration, conflict, anxiety, and identify situations that produce each one.

3. Identify the five basic sources of frustration.

4. Give examples of each of the following: approach/approach conflict; avoidance/avoidance conflict; approach/avoidance conflict; double approach/avoidance conflict.

5. Distinguish between direct coping and defensive coping.

6. Identify and characterize the three ways that people cope directly.

7. Describe all of the defense mechanisms.

8. Discuss the psychological and physiological effects of stress on people.

9. Identify five sources of extreme stress.

10. Discuss the opposing views of what characterizes a well-adjusted individual.

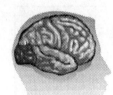

Short Essay Questions

Write out your answers to the following four essay questions to further your mastery of the topics.

1.   Online follow-up: Explain how the degree of anxiety varies with different phenomena.

_____

_____

_____

_____

_____

_____

_____

_____

_____

_____

2.   Describe three direct coping methods and two methods of defensive coping.

_____

_____

_____

_____

_____

_____

_____

_____

_____

_____

3.   Discuss the role of irrational thinking on stress.

_____

_____

_____

_____

_____

_____

_____

_____

_____

_____

4.   List the three criteria proposed by Coleman for evaluating healthy adjustment.

_____

_____

_____

_____

_____

_____

_____

_____

_____

_____

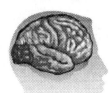

Language Support

Students identified the following words from the text as needing more explanation. This page can be cut-out, folded in half, and used as a bookmark for this chapter.

A

alleviating	getting rid of
ambivalent	not to care
annoyance	something that bothers us
apathetic	do not care

B

baseball runner	a person who is running to a base in the game of baseball

C

captors	persons holding hostages
cherish	enjoy a lot
collapse	fall
component	part
controversy	disagreement
conventionally	like most other people do it
coupled with	together with

D

debating team	a team at school that practices speaking for or against topics
desperate	frantic; last try
disastrous	very bad
dissecting	cutting apart

E

endured	lived through
exhausting	very tiring
exploding in rage	violent anger
extravagantly	an extreme amount

F

fatigue	being tired
forbidden	are not allowed to do

G

girder	a beam used to make some buildings
gracious	giving and kind

H

hostage	someone held against their will by criminals

L

looms	stands in the way

M

mobilize	to get together

O

obstacle	something you have to get over
overly optimistic	see only the good side of something when they should also be seeing the bad side

P
| perched | sitting on top of |
| procrastination | put things off until later |

R
restraint	calm behavior
rid	eliminate
ruthless	not caring if others are hurt

S
| self-assurance | good feelings about ability |
| survivors | people who live through something bad |

T
| trivial | small and not important |

U
ubiquitous	everywhere
unrealistic	not possible
utterly	totally

V
| vacillation | changing back and forth |

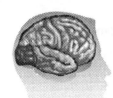

Multiple Choice Posttest

After studying the text and completing the Study Guide activities, answer these questions to determine if you need to review any areas before the course exam.

1. Kobasa described hardiness as a trait in which _____.
   a. authoritative parenting has led to greater levels of resistance to stress
   b. our experience of stress is affected by heredity
   c. people experience difficult environmental demands as challenging rather than threatening
   d. people react to conflict in a hard way

2. Deciding on a more realistic solution to a problem when an ideal solution does not seem to be possible is called _____.
   a. confrontation
   b. withdrawal
   c. aggression
   d. compromise

3. Using withdrawal as a way of coping may create future problems in that it will _____.
   a. result in denial
   b. result in avoidance of similar future situations
   c. result in aggressive actions
   d. eliminate the chance for future compromise

4. John refuses to admit he has a problem with procrastination, even though his procrastination is creating many problems in his life. John is using _____ to cope with his problem.
   a. denial
   b. sublimation
   c. projection
   d. displacement

5. You are out on a date and when something embarrassing happens your date throws a childish fit. Your date is exhibiting _____.
   a. sublimation
   b. reaction formation
   c. repression
   d. regression

6. People exhibit _____ when they express exaggerated emotions and ideas that are the opposite of their real emotions.
   a. reaction formation
   b. intellectualization
   c. repression
   d. displacement

7. You get yelled at by your boss and come home and yell at your roommate. You are using the defense mechanism of _____.
   a. reaction formation
   b. intellectualization
   c. repression
   d. displacement

8. Defense mechanisms are used by all people, however, they become a problem when they _____.
   a. lead to superstitious behavior
   b. interfere with a person's ability to function
   c. protect feelings of self-worth
   d. are used too much

9. When people are being held captive they sometimes imitate the behaviors of their captors. The prisoner's behavior is probably due to _____.
   a. reaction formation
   b. intellectualization
   c. identification
   d. displacement

10. If parents are overprotective of a child they did not want, they may be exhibiting _____.
    a. reaction formation
    b. intellectualization
    c. repression
    d. displacement

11. People who respond to life events in an intense, time urgent manner are exhibiting a _____ behavior pattern.
    a. Type A   c. Type E
    b. Type B   d. Type S

12. The incidence of _____ has been shown to increase in mice that are exposed to stressful noise.
   a. hypertension
   b. heart disease
   c. stomach ulcers
   d. cancer

13. A person's first reaction to a disaster is _____.
   a. despair
   b. confusion
   c. shock
   d. anger

14. When stressful events in the past result in anxiety, sleeplessness, and nightmares, a psychological disorder called _____ might be occurring.
   a. generalized anxiety disorder
   b. panic disorder
   c. posttraumatic stress disorder
   e. narcoleptic disorder

15. When people are well-adjusted they probably have _____.
   a. learned to get what they need regardless of what others want
   b. learned to balance conformity and nonconformity as well as self-control and spontaneity
   c. few problems
   d. none of the above

16. All of the following criteria are listed in the text as ways of evaluating adjustment EXCEPT _____.
   a. Does the action meet the individual's needs?
   b. Does the action meet the demand to adjust or does it simply postpone resolving the problem?
   c. Does the action conform to society's norms?
   d. Is the action compatible with the well-being of others?

Answers and Explanations to Multiple Choice Posttest

1. c.
2. d.
3. b.
4. a.   When we refuse to admit a problem we are denying it.
5. d.
6. a.
7. d.   Displacement is taking your anger out on someone other than the person who made you angry.
8. b.
9. c.
10. a.
11. a.
12. d.
13. c.
14. c.
15. b.
16. c.

Key Vocabulary Terms

Cut-out each term and use as study cards.
Definition is on the backside of each term.

Stress	Avoidance/ avoidance conflict
Adjustment	Approach/ avoidance conflict
Health psychology	Confrontation
Pressure	Compromise
Frustration	Withdrawal
Conflict	Defense mechanisms
Approach/ approach conflict	Denial

According to Lewin, the result of facing a choice between two undesirable possibilities, neither of which has any positive qualities.	Any environmental demand that creates a state of tension or threat and requires change or adaptation.
According to Lewin, the result of being simultaneously attracted to and repelled by the same goal.	Any effort to cope with stress.
Acknowledging a stressful situation directly and attempting to find a solution to the problem or attain the difficult goal.	A subfield within psychology concerned with the relationship between psychological factors and physical health and illness.
Deciding on a more realistic solution or goal when an ideal solution or goal is not practical.	A feeling that one must speed up, intensify, or change the direction of one's behavior or live up to a higher standard of performance.
Avoiding a situation when other forms of coping are not practical.	The feeling that occurs when a person is prevented from reaching a goal.
Self-deceptive techniques for reducing stress, including denial, repression, projection, identification, regression, intellectualization, reaction formation, displacement, and sublimation.	Simultaneous existence of incompatible demands, opportunities, needs, or goals.
Refusal to acknowledge a painful or threatening reality.	According to Lewin the result of simultaneous attraction to two appealing possibilities, neither of which has any negative qualities.

Repression	Sublimation
Projection	General adaptation syndrome
Identification	Psychoneuro-immunology
Regression	Posttraumatic stress disorder
Intellectualization	
Reaction formation	
Displacement	

Redirecting repressed motives and feelings into more socially acceptable channels.	Excluding uncomfortable thoughts, feelings, and desires from consciousness.
According to Selye, the three stages the body passes through as it adapts to stress: alarm reaction, resistance, and exhaustion.	Attributing one's own repressed motives, feelings, or wishes to others.
A field of medicine that studies the interaction between stress on the one hand and immune, endocrine, and nervous system activity on the other.	Taking on the characteristics of someone else to avoid feeling incompetent.
Psychological disorder characterized by episodes of anxiety, sleeplessness, and nightmares resulting from some disturbing event in the past.	Reverting to childlike behavior and defenses.
	Thinking abstractly about stressful problems as a way of detaching oneself from the problem.
	Expression of exaggerated ideas and emotions that are the opposite of one's repressed beliefs or feelings.
	Shifting repressed motives and emotions from an original object to a substitute object.

Overview

ABNORMAL BEHAVIOR

12

Class and Text Notes

This outline provides a way to organize your notes from both the text and the lecture. It will also serve as review sheets for the exam.

Societal, Individual, and Mental-Health Perspectives on Abnormal Behavior

Categories and Dimensions of Abnormal Behavior

Historical Views of Abnormal Behavior

Conflicting Theories of the Nature, Causes, and Treatment of Abnormal Behavior

The Biological Model

The Psychoanalytic Model

The Cognitive-Behavioral Model

The Diathesis-Stress Model and Systems Theory

Classifying Abnormal Behavior

Mood Disorders

Causes of Mood Disorders

Anxiety Disorders

Causes of Anxiety Disorders

Psychosomatic Disorders

Somatoform Disorders

Dissociative Disorders

Sexual Disorders

Sexual Dysfunction

Personality Disorders

Schizophrenic Disorders

Gender Differences in Abnormal Behavior

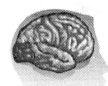

Multiple Choice Pretest

This pretest will help you identify the topics in the chapter that are most difficult for you. By focusing your study time in those areas, you will see the greatest improvement.

1. Which of the following statements is true?
   a. In recent years, psychologists and mental health professional have been able to arrive at a single definition of normal or abnormal behavior.
   b. The mental health professional's concern is whether the individual's behavior conforms to the existing social order.
   c. Defining behavior as normal or abnormal depends on whose standards and system of values are used.
   d. The definitions of normal or abnormal behavior must come from the mental health professional.

2. The _____ view of mental illness dominated nearly all early societies.
   a. psychological
   b. naturalistic
   c. philosophical
   d. supernatural

3. During the Middle Ages many people believed abnormal behavior resulted from supernatural forces and that the treatment of choice was _____.
   a. exorcism
   b. herbal cures
   c. purging with leeches
   d. magic potions

4. Early asylums were _____.
   a. primitive, but using relatively effective treatment
   b. places of human care, although they had no formal methods of treating mental illness
   c. reserved only for the rich who were mentally ill
   d. basically prisons

5. The _____ explanation of mental illness states that abnormal behavior is caused by physical malfunction that can sometimes be genetic.
   a. psychodynamic
   b. biological
   c. naturalistic
   d. cognitive-behavioral

6. The _____ model of mental illness states that abnormal behavior is caused by unconscious conflicts.
   a. psychoanalytic
   b. biological
   c. naturalistic
   d. cognitive-behavioral

7. Sarah has an extreme fear of public speaking that is interfering with her job. Her psychologist believes that the fear is learned and can be unlearned with appropriate reinforcement. This view is typical of the _____ model.
   a. psychodynamic
   b. biological
   c. naturalistic
   d. behavioral

8. Elaina is very depressed and has self-defeating beliefs. Her therapist states that her depression is caused by her negative thinking. This view is typical of the _____ model.
   a. biological
   b. cognitive
   c. behavioral
   d. psychoanalytic

9. The view that heart disease results from a combination of genetic predisposition, stress, certain personality styles, poor health behaviors, and competitive pressure is typical of the _____ approach to abnormal behavior.
   a. multimodal
   b. psychoneuroimmunological
   c. eclectic
   d. systems

10. Diathesis is thought to be a _____.
    a. split personality
    b. mental weakness
    c. physical disability
    d. biological predisposition

11. Mental disorders are categorized according to _____ in the DSM-IV.
    a. family histories
    b. biological cause of disruptive behavior
    c. significant behavior patterns
    d. specific theoretical approaches

12. Psychologists use the term "affect" to refer to _____.
    a. emotion
    b. intuition
    c. thought
    d. behavior

13. When people are _____ they have lost touch with reality.
    a. manic
    b. neurotic
    c. psychotic
    d. psychopathic

14. The symptoms of _____ include excessive excitement, fast speech followed by times of extreme sadness.
    a. dysthymia
    b. mania
    c. bipolar disorder
    d. conversion disorder

15. Eileen has an intense fear of airplanes. She is probably experiencing a _____ disorder.
    a. panic
    b. generalized anxiety
    c. conversion
    d. phobic

16. The disorder previously known as "multiple personality disorder" is now known as _____.
    a. dissociative amnesia
    b. dissociative identity disorder
    c. dissociative fugue
    d. depersonalization disorder

Answers to Multiple Choice Pretest

1. c.
2. d.
3. a.
4. d.
5. b.
6. a.
7. d.
8. b.
9. d.
10. d.
11. c.
12. a.
13. c.
14. c.
15. d.
16. b.

Learning Objectives

After you have read and studied this chapter, you should be able to complete the following statements. Your exam is written based on these learning objectives.

1. Distinguish among the standards for defining abnormal behavior from the view of society, the individual, and the mental health professional.

2. Summarize historical attitudes toward abnormal behavior.

3. State the four current models of abnormal behavior and explain the diasthesis-stress model.

4. Explain how the DSM-IV classifies mental disorders.

5. Distinguish between the two basic kinds of affective disorders and how they may interact with each other.

6. Describe and compare the anxiety disorder.

7. Recognize the characteristics of the psychophysiological disorders and the somatoform disorders.

8. Characterize three different types of dissociative disorders.

9. Define and give examples of the sexual disorders.

10. Define personality disorders. Describe four kinds of personality disorders.

11. Describe four types of schizophrenic disorders and identify possible causes of the disorder.

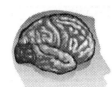

Short Essay Questions

Write out your answers to the following eight essay questions to further your mastery of the topics.

1. Online follow-up: Is the insanity defense ever valid?

_____

_____

_____

_____

_____

_____

_____

_____

_____

_____

_____

_____

_____

2. Compare and contrast four current views of abnormal behavior.

_____

_____

_____

_____

_____

_____

_____

_____

_____

_____

3. Describe the symptoms and causes of psychosomatic disorders.

_____

_____

_____

_____

_____

_____

_____

_____

_____

_____

_____

_____

_____

4. Summarize current efforts to classify abnormal behavior.

_____

_____

_____

_____

_____

_____

_____

_____

_____

_____

5. Compare and contrast simple phobias, social phobias, and agoraphobia.

_____

_____

_____

_____

_____

_____

_____

_____

_____

_____

_____

6. Discuss whether abnormal behavior should be viewed in terms of dimensions or categories.

_____

_____

_____

_____

_____

_____

_____

_____

_____

_____

_____

7. Discuss three different types of sexual dysfunction.

_____

_____

_____

_____

_____

_____

_____

_____

_____

_____

_____

8. Explain three symptoms of schizophrenic disorders.

_____

_____

_____

_____

_____

_____

_____

_____

_____

_____

_____

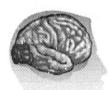

Language Support

Students identified the following words from the text as needing more explanation. This page can be cut-out, folded in half, and used as a bookmark for this chapter.

A
apathetic   not caring
appealing   interesting, likable
apprehensiveness   worried that something bad is going to happen
arbitrary   uncertain, changeable
B
blithe   cheerful
bolster   build up
brilliant   very smart
C
captured   got
causative   that which causes
chiefly   mainly
cluster   group
coexist   to be at the same time
considerable   a lot
criterion   standard
cynicism   doubt
D
debilitating   destructive; interfering
dismaying   upsetting
disobedient   not following rules
disparaging   negative
distinct   separate
dubious   questionable
E
eccentric   very unusual; odd
emerged   came out
enduring   lasting
entitlement   supposed to have
exemplifies   is an example of
exhilarated   very happy
exploit   take advantage of unfairly
F
facsimiles   to look similar to
faked   pretend
fanciful   not serious
fruitfully   successfully
full-blown   fully
G
genuinely   truly
grimacing   facial expression of pain
H
horrifying   very bad
humiliating   very embarrassing
hypervigilance   too alert

I
ideology	organized ideas
impassive	won't move
inadequate	not enough
incoherence	not able to be understood
incompetence	not skilled
incomprehensible	cannot be understood
inner distress	feel bad inside
intended	meant to be
invulnerable	cannot be hurt

J
| jittery | nervous |

L
| legitimate | real |

M
maladaptive	does not work
mannerisms	facial expressions and body movements
melancholy	sad
momentum	energy; movement

N
| nurture | environmental influence |

O
| obliged | forced to |

P
painstakingly	very carefully
plagued with	having a problem with
potpourri	mixture of many different types
promiscuity	having sexual relationships which are outside of cultural norms

R
readily	easily
resurface	come out again
reverted	went back to
rival gang	group of young people who are against the other group

S-T
scaffolding	boards and braces that workers stand on to build things high in the air
scarcity	not enough
shed some light on	explain
social deviance	not acting the way society think they should
spectrum	range
stew	think about and be upset
sweeping conclusions	broad decisions
territory	area
timid	shy
trivial	small and not important
tyrannical	not fair, very controlling

U-V-W
unconventional	not usual
unrealistically	not with what is real
vindictiveness	wanting to get back at people
vital	very important
wrenching	very painful

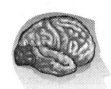

Multiple Choice Posttest

After studying the text and completing the Study Guide activities, answer these questions to determine if you need to review any areas before the course exam.

1. Which of the following is NOT a sexual disorder listed by the DSM-IV?
   a. sexual dysfunction
   b. paraphilias
   c. gender identity disorder
   d. sexual orientation disorder

2. The DSM-IV is a classification system for mental disorders that was developed by the _____.
   a. American Psychiatric Association
   b. American Psychological Association
   c. National Institute for Mental Health.
   d. American Medical Association

3. An obsession is an unwanted _____.
   a. emotion
   b. thought
   c. behavior
   d. phobia

4. What may a person experience during a panic attack?
   a. overwhelming anxiety
   b. palpitations
   c. choking sensations
   d. all of the above

5. Which of the following is NOT a cause of major depression and bipolar disorder?
   a. genetic predisposition
   b. imbalance in neurotransmitters
   b. turning hostility inward
   d. excessive dopamine

6. A person who seems withdrawn, unfeeling and distant would probably be diagnosed with a(n) _____ personality disorder.
   a. narcissistic
   b. schizoid
   c. paranoid
   d. antisocial

7. _____ disorders are inflexible and maladaptive ways of thinking and acting that are so exaggerated that they cause serious distress and social problems.
   a. Somatoform
   b. Manic
   c. Affective
   d. Personality

8. Nicole thinks of herself as extremely beautiful and intelligent. She always wants to be the center of attention. Nicole probably has a _____ personality.
   a. histrionic
   b. paranoid
   c. schizoid
   d. narcissistic

9. A personality disorder characterized by marked instability in self-image, mood, and interpersonal relationships is _____ personality disorder.
   a. borderline
   b. narcissistic
   c. antisocial
   d. schizoid

10. People exhibiting a(n) _____ personality disorder lie, steal, show no sense of responsibility, and no guilt for their behavior.
    a. borderline
    b. schizoid
    c. antisocial
    d. paranoid

11. A research study indicated that _____ percent of the populations in two prisons are antisocial personalities.
    a. 25
    b. 50
    c. 60
    d. 80

12. Disorders of inappropriate emotions, bizarre behaviors and thoughts are called
_____.
    a. sexual dysfunctions
    b. dissociative
    c. somatoform
    d. schizophrenic

13. Severe problems of motor activity is a primary feature of _____ schizophrenia.
    a. disorganized
    b. undifferentiated
    c. catatonic
    d. paranoid

14. Extreme suspiciousness is seen in _____ schizophrenia.
    a. disorganized
    b. undifferentiated
    c. catatonic
    d. paranoid

15. Excessive amounts of the neurotransmitter _____ may increase a person's predisposition to schizophrenia.
    a. serotonin
    b. norepinephrine
    c. dopamine
    d. acetylcholine

16. Mark is in constant motion and very easily distracted. He probably has _____.
    a. dysmorphic disorder
    b. attention-deficit hyperactivity disorder
    c. childhood autism
    d. reticular formation developmental disorder

17. _____ psychiatrists interview defendents in court to determine if they are mentally fit to stand trial.
    a. Prosecuint
    b. Diagnostic
    c. Developmental
    d. Forensic

18. People considering suicide usually feel very
_____.
    a. bitter
    b. apathy
    c. hopeless
    d. dissociated

Answers and Explanations to Multiple Choice Posttest

1. d. Sexual orientation is not included as a sexual disorder in DSM-IV.
2. a.
3. b.
4. d.
5. d.
6. b.
7. d.
8. d.
9. a.
10. c.
11. b.
12. d.
13. c.
14. d.
15. c.
16. b.
17. d.
18. c.

Categorical approach to classification	Systems approach
Dimensional approach to classification	Mood disorders
Biological model	Depression
Psychoanalytic model	Psychotic
Cognitive-behavioral model	Mania
Diathesis-stress model	Bipolar disorder
Diathesis	Cognitive distortions

View that biological, psychological, and social risk factors combine to produce psychological disorders. Also known as the biopsychosocial model of abnormal behavior.	Dividing mental health and mental illness into categories that are qualitatively different from one another.
Disturbances in mood or prolonged emotional state.	Viewing abnormal behavior as quantitatively different from normal behavior.
A mood disorder characterized by overwhelming feelings of sadness, lack of interest in activities, and perhaps excessive guilt or feelings of worthlessness.	View that abnormal behavior has a biochemical or physiological basis.
Marked by defective or lost contact with reality.	View that abnormal behavior is the result of unconscious internal conflicts.
A mood disorder characterized by euphoric states, extreme physical activity, excessive talkativeness, distractedness, and sometimes grandiosity.	View that abnormal behavior is the result of learning maladaptive ways of thinking.
A mood disorder in which periods of mania and depression alternate, sometimes with periods of normal mood intervening.	View that people biologically predisposed to a mental disorder (those with a certain diathesis) will tend to exhibit that disorder when particularly affected by stress.
A maladaptive response to early negative life events that leads to feelings of incompetence and unworthiness that are reactivated whenever a new situation arises that resembles the original events.	Biological predisposition.

Anxiety disorders	Psychosomatic disorders
Specific phobia	Somatoform disorders
Social phobia	Somatization disorder
Agoraphobia	Conversion disorders
Panic disorder	Hypochondriasis
Generalized anxiety disorder	Body dysmorphic disorder
Obsessive-compulsive disorder	Dissociative disorders

Disorders in which there is real physical illness that is largely caused by psychological factors such as stress and anxiety.	Disorders in which anxiety is a characteristic feature or the avoidance of anxiety seems to motivate abnormal behavior.
Disorders in which there is an apparent physical illness for which there is no organic basis.	Anxiety disorder characterized by intense, paralyzing fear of something.
A somatoform disorder characterized by recurrent vague somatic complaints without a physical cause.	An anxiety disorder characterized by excessive, inappropriate fears connected with social situations or performances in front of other people.
Somatoform disorders in which a dramatic specific disability has no physical cause but instead seems related to psychological problems.	An anxiety disorder that involves multiple, intense fear of crowds, public places, and other situations that require separation from a source of security such as the home.
A somatoform disorder in which a person interprets insignificant symptoms as signs of serious illness in the absence of any organic evidence of such illness.	An anxiety disorder characterized by recurrent panic attacks in which the person suddenly experiences intense fear or terror without any reasonable cause.
A somatoform disorder in which a person becomes so preoccupied with his or her imagined ugliness that normal life is impossible.	An anxiety disorder characterized by prolonged vague but intense fears that are not attached to any particular object or circumstance.
Disorders in which some aspect of the personality seems separated from the rest.	An anxiety disorder in which a person feels driven to think disturbing thoughts and/or to perform senseless rituals.

Dissociative amnesia	Sexual desire disorders
Dissociative fugue	Orgasm
Dissociative identity disorder	Orgasmic disorders
Depersonalization disorder	Premature ejaculation
Sexual dysfunction	Vaginismus
Erectile disorder	Personality disorders
Female sexual arousal disorder	Schizoid personality disorder

Disorders in which the person lacks sexual interest or has an active distaste for sex.	A dissociative disorder characterized by loss of memory for past events without organic cause.
Peaking of sexual pleasure and release of sexual tension.	A dissociative disorder that involves flight from home and the assumption of a new identity, with amnesia for past identity and events.
Inability to reach orgasm in a person able to experience sexual desire and maintain arousal.	A dissociative disorder in which a person has several distinct personalities that emerge at different times.
Inability of a man to inhibit orgasm as long as desired.	A dissociative disorder whose essential feature is that the person suddenly feels changed or different in a strange way.
Involuntary muscle spasms in the outer part of the vagina that make intercourse impossible.	Loss or impairment of the ordinary physical responses of sexual function.
Disorders in which inflexible and maladaptive ways of thinking and behaving learned early in life cause distress to the person and/or conflicts with others.	The inability of a man to achieve or maintain an erection.
Personality disorder in which a person is withdrawn and lacks feelings for others.	The inability of a woman to become sexually aroused or to reach orgasm.

Paranoid personality disorder	Psychotic
Dependent personality disorder	Insanity
Avoidant personality disorder	Hallucinations
Narcissistic personality disorder	Delusions
Borderline personality disorder	Disorganized schizophrenia
Antisocial personality disorder	Catatonic schizophrenia
Schizophrenic disorders	Paranoid schizophrenia

Out of touch with reality.	Personality disorder in which the person is inappropriately suspicious and mistrustful of others.
Legal term for mentally disturbed people who are not considered responsible for their criminal actions.	Personality disorder in which the person is unable to make choices and decisions independently and cannot tolerate being alone.
Sensory experiences in the absence of external stimulation.	Personality disorder in which the person's fears of rejection by others leads to social isolation.
False beliefs about reality that have no basis in fact.	Personality disorder in which the person has an exaggerated sense of self-importance and needs constant admiration.
Schizophrenic disorder in which bizarre and childlike behaviors are common.	Personality disorder characterized by marked instability in self-image, mood, and interpersonal relationships.
Schizophrenic disorder in which disturbed motor behavior is prominent.	Personality disorder that involves a pattern of violent, criminal, or unethical and exploitative behavior and an inability to feel affection for others.
Schizophrenic disorder marked by extreme suspiciousness and com	Severe disorder in which there are disturbances of thoughts, communications, and emotions, including delusions and hallucinations.

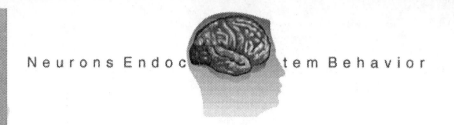

Neurons Endoctem Behavior

Overview

∙∙

Insight Therapies
Psychoanalysis
Client-Centered Therapy
Recent Developments

Behavior Therapies

Classical Conditioning
Modeling

Cognitive Therapies
Stress-Inoculation Therapy
Rational-Emotive Therapy
Beck's Cognitive Therapy

Group Therapies
Family Therapy
Marital Therapy

Effectiveness of Psychotherapy
Effectiveness of Various Forms of
    Psychotherapy

Biological Treatments
Drug Therapies
Electroconvulsive Therapy
Psychosurgery

Institutionalization

Alternative to Institutionalization
Deinstitutionalization
Alternative Forms of Treatment
Prevention

Gender Differences in Treatment

Cultural Difference in Treatment

THERAPIES

13

....

Class and Text Notes

This outline provides a way to organize your notes from both the text and the lecture. It will also serve as review sheets for the exam.

Insight Therapies

    Psychoanalysis

    Client-Centered Therapy

    Recent Developments

Behavior Therapies

Classical conditioning

Modeling

Cognitive Therapies

Stress-Inoculation Therapy

Rational-Emotive Therapy

Beck's Cognitive Therapy

Group Therapies

Family Therapy

Marital Therapy

Effectiveness of Psychotherapy

Effectiveness of Various Forms of Psychotherapy

Biological Treatments

Drug Therapies

Electroconvulsive Therapy

Psychosurgery

Institutionalization

Alternative to Institutionalization

Deinstitutionalization

Alternative Forms of Treatment

Prevention

Gender Differences in Treatment

Cultural Difference in Treatment

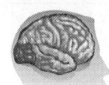

Multiple Choice Pretest

This pretest will help you identify the topics in the chapter that are most difficult for you. By focusing your study time in those areas, you will see the greatest improvement.

1. Many therapists today _____.
   a. use the humanistic approach
   b. use the psychoanalytic approach
   c. use the behavioral approach
   d. do not use only one approach

2. Insight therapies focus on giving people _____.
   a. skills to change their behaviors
   b. clearer understanding of their feelings, motives, an actions
   c. an understanding of perceptual processes
   d. an understanding of biological influences on behavior

3. Which of the following is NOT a type of insight therapy?
   a. client-centered therapy
   b. psychoanalysis
   c. insight therapy
   d. cognitive therapy

4. _____ is a technique in psychoanalysis where the patient lets his thoughts flow without interruption or inhibition.
   a. Positive transference
   b. Regression
   c. Free association
   d. Catharsis

5. A very important component of client-centered therapy is for the therapist to express _____ for the patient.
   a. psychological congruence
   b. unconditional positive regard
   c. positive transference
   d. conditional positive regard

6. In Gestalt therapy, the therapist is _____ and _____.
   a. active; directive
   b. passive; nondirective
   c. passive; directive
   d. active; nondirective

7. _____ therapists rely heavily on principles of conditioning and observational learning.
   a. Psychoanalytical
   b. Behavioral
   c. Person-centered
   d. Insight

8. A recent study found that _____ of patients showed improvements after only eight therapy sessions.
   a. 25%
   b. 50%
   c. 75%
   d. 100%

9. The focus of behavioral therapist is to _____.
   a. get the patient to look past the problem
   b. provide a warm atmosphere for discussing problems
   c. teach a client more satisfying ways of behaving
   d. provide insight into the causes of the problem

10. The technique of _____ trains a client to remain relaxed and calm in the presence of a stimulus which he or she formerly feared.
    a. reciprocal inhibition
    b. free association
    c. systematic desensitization
    d. operant conditioning

11. What therapy uses real physical pain to change behavior?
    a. aversive conditioning
    b. psychoanalysis
    c. desensitization
    d. operant conditioning

12. What therapy uses reinforcement to change behavior?
    a. aversive conditioning
    b. psychoanalysis
    c. desensitization
    d. operant conditioning

13. A therapist believes that her client suffers from misconceptions about himself and his relationship to this environment based on unrealistic expectations of himself. The focus of therapy is to change the client's beliefs into more rational ones. The therapist probably is using _____ therapy techniques.
    a. client-centered
    b. rational-emotive
    c. psychoanalytic
    d. Gestalt

14. Which of the following is an advantage of group therapy?
    a. the client has the experience of interacting with other people in a therapeutic setting
    b. it often reveals a client's problems more quickly than individual therapy
    c. it can be cheaper than individual therapy
    d. All of the above

15. Smith and Glass (1977) reported that a client receiving therapy is better off than _____ percent of untreated control subjects.
    a. 25%
    b. 50%
    c. 75%
    d. 100%

16. There is a trend among psychotherapists to combine treatment techniques in what is called _____.
    a. eclecticism
    b. humanistic therapy
    c. group treatment
    d. behavior therapy

17. Only _____ are licensed to give drug therapy.
    a. counselors
    b. psychologists
    c. psychiatrists
    d. therapists

Answers to Multiple Choice Pretest

1. d.
2. b.
3. d.
4. c.
5. b.
6. a.
7. b.
8. b.
9. c.
10. c.
11. a.
12. d.
13. b.
14. d.
15. c.
16. a.
17. c.

Learning Objectives

After you have read and studied this chapter, you should be able to complete the following statements. Your exam is written based on these learning objectives.

1. Differentiate between insight therapies, behavior therapies, cognitive therapies, and group therapies.

2. Discuss the criticisms of psychoanalysis.

3. Explain how client-centered and rational-emotive therapists interpret causes of emotional problems. Describe the therapeutic techniques of each approach.

4. Summarize the behavioral therapist's interpretation of disorders. Describe aversive conditioning, desensitization, and modeling.

5. Describe stress-inoculation therapy, Beck's cognitive therapy, and Gestalt therapy.

6. List the advantages and disadvantages of group therapies. Identify five current approaches to group therapy.

7. Discuss the effectiveness of insight therapy and behavior therapy.

8. Outline the available biological treatments and discuss the advantages and disadvantages of each.

9. Summarize the inadequacies of institutionalization. List the alternative to institutionalization.

10. Explain the differences between primary, secondary, and tertiary prevention.

11. Discuss possible areas of misunderstanding when there are cultural differences in therapy.

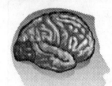

Short Essay Questions

Write out your answers to the following four essay questions to further your mastery of the topics.

1.   Online follow-up: Are biological treatments like psychosurgery and ECT ever justified?

_____

_____

_____

_____

_____

_____

_____

_____

_____

_____

_____

2.   Summarize the research on the effectiveness of various types of psychotherapy.

_____

_____

_____

_____

_____

_____

_____

_____

_____

_____

_____

3.   Describe the advantages and goals of group therapy. Identify two types of group therapy.

_____

_____

_____

_____

_____

_____

_____

_____

_____

_____

_____

4.   Compare the advantages and disadvantages of institutionalization/ deinstitutionalization.

_____

_____

_____

_____

_____

_____

_____

_____

_____

_____

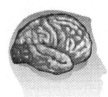

Language Support

Students identified the following words from the text as needing more explanation. This page can be cut-out, folded in half, and used as a bookmark for this chapter.

A
abstinence   do not do the behavior
accurate   true
adage   saying
advent   beginning
alleviating   get rid of
ambulatory   people are able to walk
C
cardinal rule   most important rule
clam up   stop talking
coarsening   getting rougher and not as nice
commonsense   logical; understandable to many people
constrained   held back
D
derogatory   negative
E
edgewise   in between
emphatically   very strongly
enhancing   increasing
enviable   something others want
establishment   starting
exemplify   show
extent   amount
F
fraught with   troubled by
H
hodgepodge   confusing mixture
I
inconsistent   does not stay the same
L
lurk   stay hidden
M
makeshift   thrown together quickly and not carefully
manifest   seen
mere   only
O
overbearing   too strong and controlling
P
prognosis   likely future changes in the disorder (problem)
proliferation   growth; large increase
R
restore   get back
revelations   explanations that tell new information
rigidity   stiffness

S
self-perpetuating	tends to continue by itself
simultaneously	at the same time
social stigma	looked down on by other people
spiral	spread out into
stroke	pet

T
tarantula	very large spider
testify	to make a strong statement
transition	change
treatment modality	way of treating

U
| underfunded | not enough money |
| underscores | emphasizes |

V
| vehemently | very strongly |

W
| warehouses for victims | large buildings in which people with mental disorders live |
| wariness | fearfulness |

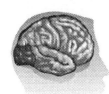

Multiple Choice Posttest

After studying the text and completing the Study Guide activities, answer these questions to determine if you need to review any areas before the course exam.

1. Often the techniques used by therapists today utilize_____.
   a. the humanistic approach
   b. the psychoanalytic approach
   c. the behavioral approach
   d. not just one approach

2. Insight therapies focus on giving people _____.
   a. skills to change their behaviors
   b. clearer understanding of their feelings, motives, an actions
   c. an understanding of perceptual processes
   d. an understanding of biological influences on behavior

3. All of the following are insight therapies EXCEPT _____.
   a. client-centered therapy
   b. psychoanalysis
   c. insight therapy
   d. cognitive therapy

4. _____ is very important component of client-centered therapy.
   a. Psychological congruence
   b. Unconditional positive regard
   c. Positive transference
   d. Conditional positive regard

5. All of the following are biological therapies EXCEPT _____.
   a. RET
   b. ECT
   c. drug therapy
   d. psychosurgery

6. The main task of behavioral therapy is to _____.
   a. get the patient to look past the problem
   b. provide a warm atmosphere for discussing problems
   c. teach a client to behave in more functional ways
   d. provide insight into the causes of the problem

7. The technique of _____ trains a client to remain relaxed and calm in the presence of a stimulus which he or she formerly feared.
   a. reciprocal inhibition
   b. free association
   c. systematic desensitization
   d. operant conditioning

8. A therapist believes that her client suffers from misconceptions about himself and his relationship to this environment based on unrealistic expectations of himself. The focus of therapy is to change the client's beliefs into more rational ones. The therapist probably is using _____ therapy techniques.
   a. client-centered
   b. rational-emotive
   c. psychoanalytic
   d. Gestalt

9. _____ are mental health practitioners who are licensed to give medication.
   a. Counselors
   b. Psychologists
   c. Psychiatrists
   d. Therapists

10. Most antipsychotic drugs work by _____.
    a. increasing acetylcholine in the brain
    b. increasing serotonin in the brain
    c. inhibiting the function of the hypothalamus
    d. blocking dopamine receptors in the brain

11. "Prozac" is a medication used for _____.
    a. hallucinations
    b. depression
    c. mania
    d. psychosurgery

12. The effects of psychosurgery _____.
    a. do not include undesirable side effects
    b. are useless in controlling pain
    c. are all negative
    d. are difficult to predict

13. Electroconvulsive therapy is considered
    _____ effective in treating _____ cases of
    depression.
    a. highly; mild
    b. highly; severe
    c. slightly ; mild
    d. slightly; severe

14. Which of the following treatments is LEAST
    likely to be used today?
    a. electroconvulsive therapy
    b. drug treatment
    c. prefrontal lobotomy
    d. shock therapy

15. The focus of _____ prevention is
    intervention.
    a. basic
    b. primary
    c. secondary
    d. tertiary

16. In Native American culture, not making eye
    contact and looking downward during a
    conversation is a sign of _____.
    a. respect
    b. denigration
    c. appreciation
    d. depression

17. Alcoholics Anonymous is an example of a
    _____.
    a. psychoanalytic therapy group
    b. self-help group
    c. desensitization group
    d. structured behavior therapy group

Answers to Multiple Choice Posttest

1. d.
2. b.
3. d.
4. b.
5. a.
6. c.
7. c.
8. b.
9. c.
10. d.
11. b.
12. d.
13. b.
14. c.
15. c.
16. a.
17. b.

Key Vocabulary Terms

Cut-out each term and use as study cards.
Definition is on the backside of each term.

Psychotherapy	Gestalt therapy
Insight therapy	Short-term psycho-dynamic therapy
Psychoanalysis	Behavior therapies
Free association	Systematic desensitization
Transference	Aversive conditioning
Insight	Behavior contracting
Client-centered or person-centered	Token economy

An insight therapy that emphasizes the wholeness of the personality and attempts to reawaken people to their emotions and sensations in the here-and-now.	The use of psychological techniques to treat personality and behavior disorders.
Insight therapy that is time-limited and focused on trying to help clients correct the immediate problems in their lives.	A variety of individual psychotherapies designed to give people a better understanding of their feelings, motivations, and actions in the hope that this will help them adjust.
Therapeutic approaches that are based on the belief that all behavior, normal and abnormal, is learned, and that the objective of therapy is to teach people new, more satisfying ways of behaving.	An insight therapy developed by Freud, that is based on the belief that psychological problems are symptoms of inner conflicts repressed during childhood.
A behavioral technique for reducing a person's fear and anxiety by gradually associating a new response (relaxation) with stimuli that have been causing the fear and anxiety.	A psychoanalytic technique that encourages the patient to talk without inhibition about whatever thoughts or fantasies come to mind.
Behavior therapy techniques aimed at eliminating undesirable behavior patterns by teaching the person to associate them with pain and discomfort.	The patient's carrying over to the analyst feelings held toward childhood authority figure.
Form of operant conditioning therapy in which the client and therapist set behavioral goals and agree on reinforcements the client will receive	Awareness of previously unconscious feelings and memories and how they influence present feelings and behavior.
An operant conditioning therapy in which patients earn tokens (reinforcers) for desired behaviors and exchange them for desired items or privileges.	Nondirectional form of therapy developed by Carl Rogers that calls for unconditional positive regard of the client by the therapist with the goal of helping the client become fully functioning.

Modeling	Marital therapy
Cognitive therapies	Eclecticism
Stress-inoculation therapy	Biological treatments
Rational-emotive therapy (ET)	Antipsychotic drugs
Cognitive therapy	Electroconvulsive therapy
Group therapy	Psychosurgery
Family therapy	Deinstitutionalization

Form of group therapy intended to help troubled couples improve their problems of communication and interaction.	A behavior therapy in which the person learns desired behaviors by watching others perform those behaviors.
Psychotherapeutic approach that recognizes the value of a broad treatment package over a rigid commitment to one particular form of therapy.	Psychotherapies that emphasize changing clients' perceptions of their life situations as a way of modifying their behavior.
Group of approaches, including medication, electroconvulsive therapy, and psychosurgery, that are sometimes used to treat psychological disorders in conjunction with, or instead of, psychotherapy.	A type of cognitive therapy that trains clients to cope with stressful situations by learning a more useful pattern of self-talk.
Drugs used to treat very severe psychological disorders, particularly schizophrenia.	A directive cognitive therapy based on the idea that client's psychological distress is caused by irrational and self-defeating beliefs and that the therapist's job is to challenge such dysfunctional beliefs.
Biological therapy in which a mild electrical current is passed through the brain for a short period, often producing convulsions and temporary coma; used to treat severe, prolonged depression.	Therapy that depends on identifying and changing inappropriately negative and self-critical patterns of thought.
Brain surgery performed to change a person's behavior or emotional state; a biological therapy rarely used today.	Type of psychotherapy in which clients meet regularly to interact and help one another achieve insight into their feelings and behavior.
Policy of treating people with severe psychological disorders in the larger community, or in small residential centers such as halfway houses, rather than in large public hospitals.	A form of group therapy that sees the family as at least partly responsible for the individual's problems and that seeks to change all family members' behaviors to the benefit of the family unit as well as the troubled individual.

Prevention	
Primary prevention	
Secondary prevention	
Tertiary prevention	

	Reducing the incidence of emotional disturbance by eliminating conditions that cause or contribute to mental disorders and substituting conditions that foster mental well-being.
	Techniques and programs to improve the social environment so that new cases of mental disorders do not develop.
	Programs to identify groups that are at high risk for mental disorders and to detect maladaptive behavior and treat it promptly.
	Programs to help people adjust to community life after release from a mental hospital.

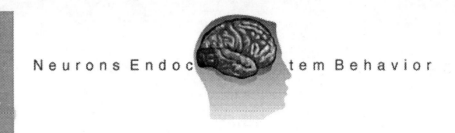

Neurons Endoc[...]tem Behavior

Overview

· ·

Social Cognition
Impression Formation
Attribution
Interpersonal Attraction

Attitudes
The Nature of Attitudes
Prejudice and Discrimination
Attitude Change

Social Influence
Cultural influence
Cultural Assimilators
Conformity
Compliance
Obedience

Social Action
Deindividuation
Helping Behavior
Group Decision Making
Organizational Behavior

SOCIAL PSYCHOLOGY

14

Class and Text Notes

This outline provides a way to organize your notes from both the text and the lecture. It will also serve as review sheets for the exam.

Social Cognition

Impression Formation

Attribution

Interpersonal Attraction

Attitudes

The Nature of Attitudes

Prejudice and Discrimination

Attitude Change

Social Influence

Cultural influence

Cultural Assimilators

Conformity

Compliance

Obedience

Social Action

Deindividuation

Helping Behavior

Group Decision Making

Organizational Behavior

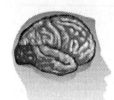

Multiple Choice Pretest

This pretest will help you identify the topics in the chapter that are most difficult for you. By focusing your study time in those areas, you will see the greatest improvement.

1. The study of the way thoughts, feelings and behaviors of a person are affected by the perceived characteristics of others is known as _____ psychology.
   a. interpersonal
   b. social
   c. environmental
   d. cognitive

2. The _____ effect occurs when our first impressions influence our opinion about someone more than current information.
   a. halo
   b. recency
   c. primacy
   d. phi phenomenon

3. When the expectation of one person influences the behavior of another person, the expectation has become a(n) _____.
   a. response characteristic
   b. primary drive
   c. attribution
   d. self-fulfilling prophecy

4. A(n) _____ is the belief that all members of a social category have the same characteristics.
   a. perception
   b. primacy effect
   c. stereotype
   d. unifying trait

5. According to Heider, we usually attribute someone's behavior to _____.
   a. internal and external causes at the same time
   b. either internal or external causes, but not both at the same time
   c. external causes only
   d. internal causes only

6. According to Jones and Nisbett, we tend to attribute our own actions to _____ factors and the behavior of others to _____ factors.

   a. situational; personal
   b. situational; situational
   c. personal; personal
   d. personal; situational

7. The _____ is when we place too much emphasis on personal factors when trying to explain other people's actions.
   a. Peter principle
   b. primacy effect
   c. fundamental attribution error
   d. defensive attribution

8. The most important factor in interpersonal attraction is _____.
   a. reciprocity   c. similarity
   b. attractiveness   d. proximity

9. Being attracted to someone because of opposite interests or personality characteristics is called _____.
   a. reciprocity
   b. complementarity
   c. rewardingness
   d. proximity

10. Liking someone who has expressed a liking for us is called _____.
    a. exchange
    b. proximity
    c. reciprocity
    d. complementarity

11. _____ is a very important part of intimate communication.
    a. Kinesics
    b. Self-disclosure
    c. Deindividuation
    d. Proxemics

12. When a person observes a situation for cues about how to react, this is called _____.
    a. situational narcissism
    b. self-efficacy
    c. reaction formation
    d. self-monitoring

13. Prejudice is to a(n) _____ as discrimination is to a(n) _____.
   a. unfavorable attitude; unfair act
   b. tolerance; oppression
   c. unfair act; unfavorable attitude
   d. oppression; tolerance

14. People who are punished for problems they
did not cause are called _____.
   a. bigots
   b. victims
   c. scapegoats
   d. egalitarian

15. The message which MOST likely will result in
a change of attitude is a message with
_____.
   a. high fear from a highly credible source
   b. high fear from a moderately credible
       source
   c. moderate fear from a highly credible
       source
   d. moderate fear from a moderately credible
       source

16. When trying to change someone's opinion, it is
generally better to _____.
   a. present only your side of an argument
   b. present only criticisms of the opposing
       viewpoint
   c. present both sides of an argument, giving
       the opposing side first
   d. present both sides of an argument, giving
       your side first

17. The most powerful method of changing
people's opinions is usually _____.
   a. a media presentation
   b. "word of mouth"
   c. personal contact
   d. a written argument

18. People with _____ are more easily influ-
enced to change their attitudes.
   a. low self-esteem
   b. high self-esteem
   c. low achievement need
   d. high achievement need

Learning Objectives

After you have read and studied this chapter, you should be able to complete the following statements. Your exam is written based on these learning objectives.

1. Describe the process by which we form first impressions of other people. Identify three factors that influence personal perception.

2. Explain three aspects of attribution and explain attribution errors.

3. Explain the dynamics of interpersonal attraction.

4. Identify the components of attitudes. Discuss the relationship between attitude and behavior.

5. Explain how attitudes are acquired.

6. Explain the origin of prejudice and discrimination and how prejudice can be reduced.

7. Discuss the dynamics of attitude change and the process of persuasion.

8. Explain the theory of cognitive dissonance. List ways to reduce cognitive dissonance.

9. Define risky shift and polarization. Summarize the conditions under which groups are effective and ineffective in solving problems.

10. Explain how culture, conformity, compliance, and obedience exert social influence.

11. Identify the four types of social action.

12. Identify the theories of leadership.

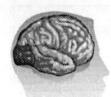

Short Essay Questions

Write out your answers to the following four essay questions to further your mastery of the topics.

1. Online follow-up: Does the norm of obedience to an authority figure alter an individual's responsibility for his or her behavior?

_____

_____

_____

_____

_____

_____

_____

_____

_____

_____

_____

_____

2. Identify and describe the factors that influence the formation of impressions about people.

_____

_____

_____

_____

_____

_____

_____

_____

_____

_____

_____

_____

3. Identify five factors that influence the effectiveness of efforts to change people's attitudes.

_____

_____

_____

_____

_____

_____

_____

_____

_____

_____

_____

_____

4. Describe the factors influencing group decision-making and the effectiveness of groups.

_____

_____

_____

_____

_____

_____

_____

_____

_____

_____

_____

_____

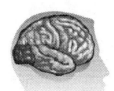

Language Support

Students identified the following words from the text as needing more explanation. This page can be cut-out, folded in half, and used as a bookmark for this chapter.

A
amiability   get along
animated   actions were full of energy
arouse   to bring up
B
beyond   further
C
candor   openness
cognitive dissonance   thinking something is not right
cohesiveness   working together well
comply   go along with
comprehend   understand
conform   go along with
consensus   everyone agrees
contradictory   do not agree
counterarguments   statements against
D
demonstrable   can be shown
depicted   shown
discrepant   not compatible
E
emerged   came out
endorsements   supporting statements
exerting   trying hard
G
genuine   real
governed   controlled
I
indecisive   cannot make a decision
L
loathing   to hate a lot
M
mystification   mystery around it
O
optimism   thinking good things will happen
P
perpetuating   making something last
persisted   lasted
persuasive   convincing
Q
quota   a certain amount that is supposed to be reached
R
rationalization   excuse
repetitive tasks   things done over and over again

S
scanty	too little
scarcely	very little
scare tactics	something designed to frighten us
simplistic	simple
speculation	guesses

U
unforeseen	not aware of before

V
vent	release

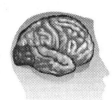

Multiple Choice Posttest

After studying the text and completing the Study Guide activities, answer these questions to determine if you need to review any areas before the course exam.

1. A behavioral rule shared by a whole society is called a _____.
   a. cultural more
   b. folkway
   c. cultural truism
   d. cultural norm

2. Laws are typically based on _____.
   a. cultural more
   b. folkway
   c. cultural truism
   d. cultural norm

3. All of the following are likely to increase an individual's conformity to group behavior EXCEPT
   a. The person is attracted to the group.
   b. The person expects to interact with the - group.
   c. The person feels accepted by the group.
   d. The person is of relatively low status in the group.

4. The _____ effect is that people are more likely to comply with a second, larger request after complying with a first, small request.
   a. response cue
   b. bait and switch
   c. foot-in-the-door
   d. primacy

5. _____ is a process by which people feel anonymous in a large group.
   a. Deindividuation
   b. Identity diffusion
   c. Identity moratorium
   d. Social facilitation

6. In a mob, one dominant person can often convince people to act due to the _____ effect.
   a. lowball
   b. snowball
   c. primacy
   d. door-in-the-face

7. _____ behavior is helping other people with no expectation of personal gain.
   a. Reciprocal
   b. Deindividuated
   c. Diffused
   d. Altruistic

8. When there is so much pressure from the group to conform that people do not feel free to express critical ideas, this is called
   _____.
   a. groupthink
   b. polarization
   c. risky shift
   d. deindividuation

9. The poor decisions made in the Watergate cover-up, the Challenger disaster and the Bay of Pigs invasion were due primarily to
   _____.
   a. groupthink
   b. polarization
   c. risky shift
   d. deindividuation

10. The focus of industrial/organizational psychology is _____.
    a. strategies for founding an economically successful business
    b. behavior in organizational settings
    c. the effects of industrialization on the environment
    d. personal problems of employed people

11. In the Mayo study of workers at the Hawthorne plant, _____.
    a. productivity improved as lighting was decreased
    b. productivity improved as lighting was increased
    c. productivity improved no matter what was done to the lighting conditions
    d. none of the above

12. Which of the following did Rempel and Holmes NOT recommend for developing and strengthening trust?
    a. focus on specific actions rather than motives
    b. focus on how to improve the person
    c. don't dwell on negative memories
    d. be fair and realistic in interpreting someone's behavior

13. Someone who falls at work is MOST likely to attribute the fall to _____.
    a. problems he is having in his personal life
    b. errors in judgment on his part
    c. a slick surface at work
    d. being distracted by thoughts about the weekend

14. The term psychologists use for how close two people live to each other is _____.
    a. propinquity
    b. proximity
    c. reciprocity
    d. complementarily

15. Rebecca consistently expresses her belief with little regard for the constraints imposed by the situation. She is probably a _____ self-monitor.
    a. reactive
    b. nonreactive
    c. low
    d. high

16. Which of the following personality types is MOST likely to be prejudiced?
    a. altruistic
    b. egalitarian
    c. authoritarian
    d. intellectual

17. Reducing racial prejudice can be best accomplished by _____.
    a. education
    b. contact
    c. competition
    d. cooperation

Answers to Multiple Choice Posttest

1. d.
2. d.
3. c.
4. c.
5. a.
6. b.
7. d.
8. a.
9. a.
10. b.
11. c.
12. b.
13. c.
14. b.
15. c.
16. c.
17. d.

Social psychology	Just-world hypothesis
Primacy effect	Proximity
Self-fulfilling prophecy	Exchange
Stereotype	Equity
Attribution theory	Intimacy
Fundamental attribution error	Attitude
Defensive attribution	Self-monitoring

Attribution error based on the assumption that bad things happen to bad people and good things happen to good people.	Scientific study of the ways in which the thoughts, feelings, and behaviors of one individual are influenced by the real, imagined, or inferred behavior or characteristics of other people.
How close two people live to each other.	Early information about someone weighs more heavily than later information in influencing one's impression of that person.
Concept that relationships are based on trading rewards among partners.	Process in which a person's expectation about another elicits behavior from the second person that confirms the expectation.
Fairness of exchange achieved when each partner in the relationship receives the same proportion of outcomes to investments.	Set of characteristics presumed to be shared by all members of a social category.
The quality of genuine closeness and trust achieved in communication with another person.	Theory that addresses the question of how people make judgments about the causes of behavior.
Relatively stable organization of beliefs, feelings, and behavior tendencies directed toward something or someone–the attitude object.	Tendency of people to overemphasize personal causes for other people's behavior and to underemphasize personal causes for their own behavior.
Tendency for an individual to observe the situation for cues about how to react.	Tendency to attribute our successes to our own efforts or qualities and our failures to external factors.

Prejudice	Cultural truism
Discrimination	Norm
Frustration-aggression theory	Cultural norm
Authoritarian personality	Conformity
Cognitive dissonance	Compliance
Social influence	Obedience
Culture	Deindividuation

Belief that most members of a society accept as self-evidently true.	An unfair, intolerant, or unfavorable attitude toward a group of people.
A shared idea or expectation about how to behave.	An unfair act or series of acts taken toward an entire group of people or individual members of that group.
A behavioral rule shared by an entire society.	Theory that under certain circumstances people who are frustrated in their goals turn their anger away from the proper, powerful target toward another, less powerful target it is safer to attack.
Voluntarily yielding to social norms, even at the expense of one's own preferences.	A personality pattern characterized by rigid conventionality, exaggerated respect for authority, and hostility toward those who defy society's norms.
Change of behavior in response to an explicit request from another person or group.	Perceived inconsistency between two cognitions.
Change of behavior in response to a command from another person, typically an authority figure.	Process by which others individually or collectively affect one's perceptions, attitudes, and actions.
Loss of personal sense of responsibility in a group.	All the goods, both tangible and intangible, produced in a society.

Altruistic behavior	
Bystander effect	
Risky shift	
Polarization	
Great person theory	
Industrial/organi- zation psychology	
Hawthorne effect	

	Helping behavior that is not linked to personal gain.
	Tendency for an individual's helpfulness in an emergency to decrease as the number of bystanders increases.
	Greater willingness to take risks in decision making in a group than as independent individuals.
	Shift in attitudes by members of a group toward more extreme positions than the ones held before group's discussion.
	Theory that leadership is a result of personal qualities and traits that qualify one to lead others.
	Division of psychology concerned with the application of psychological principles to the problems of human organizations, especially work organizations.
	Principle that subjects will alter their behavior because of researcher's attention and not necessarily because of any specific experimentation.

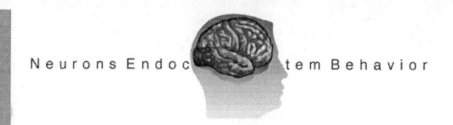

Neurons Endoc   tem Behavior

Overview

● ●

Gender Diversity
Gender Stereotypes
Gender and Cognitive Skills
Gender and Emotion
Gender and Social Behavior
Gender Diversity: Summing Up

Cultural Diversity
Race and Ethnicity
What Is a Culture?
Culture and Cognition
Categorization
Culture and Emotion
Culture and Social Behavior

HUMAN DIVERSITY

15

Class and Text Notes

This outline provides a way to organize your notes from both the text and the lecture. It will also serve as review sheets for the exam.

Gender Diversity

Gender Stereotypes

Gender and Cognitive Skills

Gender and Emotion

Gender and Social Behavior

Gender Diversity: Summing Up

Cultural Diversity

Race and Ethnicity

What Is a Culture?

Culture and Cognition

Categorization

Culture and Emotion

Culture and Social Behavior

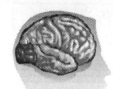

Multiple Choice Pretest

This pretest will help you identify the topics in the chapter that are most difficult for you. By focusing your study time in those areas, you will see the greatest improvement.

1. For a long-time psychological research was done using _____.
   a. male and female subjects from North America, Asia, Europe, and Africa
   b. male subjects from North America, Asia, Europe
   c. white male subjects from the United States and Western Europe
   d. male and female subjects from United States and Western Europe

2. _____ are beliefs about the characteristics that men and women are presumed to have.
   a. Gender roles
   b. Gender differences
   c. Gender norms
   d. Gender stereotypes

3. Women in most cultures take care of children and family, cook meals, and do laundry. These behaviors are examples of _____.
   a. gender roles
   b. gender stereotypes
   c. gender differences
   d. gender norms

4. In newspapers and magazines, pictures of men tend to emphasize their _____.
   a. eyes
   b. face
   c. clothes
   d. body

5. Combining the results of several independent research studies to form an overall conclusion is called _____.
   a. analysis of variance
   b. stepwise regression analysis
   c. meta-analysis
   d. factor analysis

6. Hyde's research found that in mathematical skills, males and females were equal in _____.

   a. no specific type of mathematical skills
   b. understanding mathematical concepts
   c. problem solving
   d. computation

7. Research indicates that gender differences in cognitive abilities show up in _____.
   a. neither specific cognitive abilities nor general intelligence
   b. specific cognitive abilities but not in general intelligence
   c. general intelligence but not in specific cognitive abilities
   d. specific cognitive abilities and general intelligence

8. Hall's research led her to conclude that women are _____.
   a. more skilled than men in some situations, and less skilled than men in other situations at decoding the emotional expressions of others
   b. more skilled than men at decoding the emotional expression of others
   c. less skilled than men at decoding the emotional expressions of others
   d. about equally skilled as men at decoding the emotional expression of others

9. Snodgrass has found that
   a. leaders are less sensitive than followers to the emotions of others
   b. leaders and followers are equally sensitive to the emotions of others
   c. leaders are more sensitive than followers to the emotions of others
   d. leaders are more sensitive to the emotions of other leaders than the emotions of followers

10. Jobs high in emotion labor tend to be filled by _____.
    a. men
    b. women
    c. adolescents
    d. elderly persons

11. Men are more likely than females to behave aggressively _____ cultures and at _____.
    a. across cultures; every age
    b. only in industrialized; younger ages
    c. across; younger ages
    d. only in industrialized; every age

12. Men are more likely to help in each of the following situations EXCEPT situations _____.
    a. in which the person needing help is a female
    b. in which an audience is present
    c. that call for heroism toward a stranger
    d. that require offering social support

13. Women tend to have a more _____ style of leadership than men.
    a. autocratic
    b. instrumental
    c. group-oriented
    d. laissez-faire

14. In summarizing the research on gender diversity, it is probably most accurate to say that _____.
    a. there is no variability within gender or across genders
    b. there is more variability within gender than across genders
    c. there is equal variability within gender and across genders
    d. there is more variability across genders than within genders

15. Feeling disoriented or uncertain when exposed to an unfamiliar way of life is what psychologists call _____.
    a. disequilibrium
    b. desynchronization
    c. culture shock
    d. social withdrawal

16. A common cultural heritage, including religion, and/or ancestry, that is shared by a group of individuals is called _____.
    a. ethnicity
    b. society
    c. social class
    d. race

Answers to Multiple Choice Pretest

1. c.
2. d.
3. a.
4. b.
5. c.
6. b.
7. b.
8. b.
9. a.
10. b.
11. a.
12. d.
13. c.
14. b.
15. c.
16. d.

Learning Objectives

After you have read and studied this chapter, you should be able to complete the following statements. Your exam is written based on these learning objectives.

1. Give two examples of gender stereotypes.

2. Explain the differences in cognitive skills between men and women.

3. Compare men's and women's ability to decode emotional messages.

4. Describe differences between men and women in the areas of aggression, helping, conformity, and leadership.

5. Explain the terms *cultural shock* and *ethnic identity*.

6. Explain the tangible and intangible components of culture.

7. Describe cultural differences in performing cognitive tasks.

8. Compare how emotions are experienced in individualistic and collectivistic cultures.

9. Explain differences in aggression, helping, conformity, and leadership in collectivistic as compared to individualistic cultures.

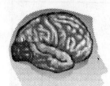

Short Essay Questions

Write out your answers to the following four essay questions to further your mastery of the topics.

1. Online follow-up: How does cultural experience affect our ability to learn things?

_____
_____
_____
_____
_____
_____
_____
_____
_____
_____
_____
_____

2. Explain what gender stereotypes and gender roles are and how they impact people's lives.

_____
_____
_____
_____
_____
_____
_____
_____
_____
_____

3. Summarize the research on gender and aggression, conformity, and leadership.

_____
_____
_____
_____
_____
_____
_____
_____
_____
_____
_____
_____

4. How do gestures, etc. vary across cultures?

_____
_____
_____
_____
_____
_____
_____
_____
_____
_____

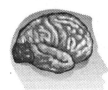

Language Support

Students identified the following words from the text as needing more explanation. This page can be cut-out, folded in half, and used as a bookmark for this chapter.

A
assimilated   brought into
B
boastful   brag about yourself
C
conflicting   do not agree with
cowherd   someone who herds cows
cultural context   the environment of a culture
curriculum   planned educational material
D
deintensify   to make less
distinguish   tell the difference between
E
emblem   symbol
exclusively   only
I
intuitive   idea that makes sense
M
maintain   keep
mask   hide
misbegotten   not thought of correctly
P
popular notion   a belief held by many people
predominantly   mainly
proneness   likely to do
pursuing   going after
R
restricted   limited
S
scarcity   too few
subpopulation   a small group of a larger group
T
transmitted   carried
U
utilized   used

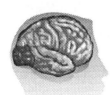

Multiple Choice Posttest

After studying the text and completing the Study Guide activities, answer these questions to determine if you need to review any areas before the course exam.

1. According to your text, culture has _____ effect on memory.
   a. virtually no
   b. one a subtle
   c. a moderate, but consistent
   d. a profound

2. Studies of first- and firth-grade American, Chinese, and Japanese students; mathematical and reading skills in 1990 found that _____.
   a. students from all three countries were essentially equal
   b. Chinese students had the best reading abilities and the best mathematical abilities
   c. Japanese students had the best mathematical abilities but the worst reading abilities
   d. American students had the worst mathematical abilities and the worst reading abilities

3. Comparisons of American and Asian schools have found that American schools have _____ variety of activities and the teachers in American schools are _____ trained in educational methods and teaching strategies.
   a. less; not as well
   b. more; not as well
   c. less better
   d. more; better

4. The process in which people tend to overestimate the internal causes of someone else's behavior is called the _____.
   a. self-serving bias
   b. primacy effect
   c. fundamental attribution error
   d. just world hypothesis

5. Which of the following emotions reflects the type of feeling words that are more commonly found in the Japanese language than in the English language?
   a. empathy
   b. happiness
   c. sadness
   d. anger

6. Among nonverbal channels of communication, _____ communicate(s) the most specific information.
   a. facial expression
   b. hand gestures
   c. eye contact
   d. posture

7. Culture-specific principles that govern how, when and why facial expressions of emotion are shown are called _____.
   a. expression laws
   b. display rules
   c. emotion labor
   d. masking principles

8. A display rule in which you mute your facial expression is called _____.
   a. masking
   b. neutralizing
   c. intensifying
   d. deintensifying

9. To be able to understand what others are feeling you _____.
   a. do not need to know either universal facial expressions nor emotion rules
   b. need to know the universal facial expressions but not emotion rules
   c. need to know emotion rules but not universal facial expressions
   d. need to know both emotion rules and universal facial expressions

10. Emblems refer to _____
    a. eye signals
    b. hand gestures
    c. facial expressions
    d. distinctive postures

11. Which of the following countries has the highest murder rate?
    a. the United States
    b. Finland
    c. Norway
    d. China

HUMAN DIVERSITY 339

12. In comparing aggressive behavior across collectivist and individualist cultures, researchers have found that _____.
    a. both collectivist and individualist cultures are relatively nonaggressive
    b. collectivist cultures are relatively nonaggressive compared to individualist cultures
    c. individualist cultures are relatively nonaggressive compared to collectivist cultures
    d. both collectivist and individualist cultures are relatively aggressive

13. Leaders and group members in collectivist cultures _____.
    a. have more specifically defined roles than in individualist cultures
    b. leaders have more clearly defined roles but group members have roles similar to those found in individualist cultures
    c. are almost identical in how their roles are defined as they are in individualist cultures
    d. leaders have less clearly defined roles than in individualist cultures

14. People living in _____ cultures emphasize self-reliance, independence, and achieving personal goals, even at the expense of the goals of a larger group.
    a. autocratic
    b. collectivist
    c. individualist
    d. paternalist

15. People living in _____ cultures emphasize the goals of their group and often strive for harmonious relationships with other group members.
    a. laissez-faire
    b. collectivist
    c. individualist
    d. industrialized

16. People living in collectivistic cultures tend to be _____.
    a. culture neutral
    b. allocentric
    c. egocentric
    d. idiocentric

17. Each of the following countries tends to have a collectivistic culture EXCEPT _____.
    a. Japan
    b. Zaire
    c. El Salvador
    d. Great Britain

Gender stereotypes	Social cognition
Gender roles	Display rules
Meta-analysis	Collectivist cultures
Culture shock	
Race	
Ethnicity	
Ethnic identity	

Knowledge and understanding concerning the social world and the people in it (including oneself).	General beliefs about characteristics that men and women are presumed to have.
Culture-specific rules that govern how, when and why facial expressions of emotion are displayed.	Behaviors that we expect each gender to engage in.
These cultures tend to have many terms for other-focused emotions and promote emotional displays that are designed to maintain group cohesion.	A way of statistically combining the results of several independent research studies to form an overall conclusion.
	Feeling disoriented or uncertain when exposed to an unfamiliar way of life.
	A subpopulation of a species, defined according to an identifiable dimension (i.e., geographic location, skin color, hair texture, genes, facial features).
	A common cultural heritage, including religion, language, and/or ancestry, that is shared by a group of individuals.
	That aspect of an individual's self-concept that is based on his or her awareness of being a member of a particular ethnic group.

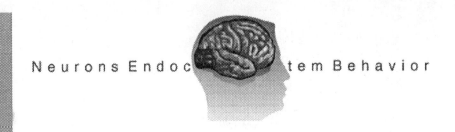

Neurons Endoc... tem Behavior

Overview

· ·

Scales of Measurement

Measurements of Central Tendency
Differences Between the Mean, Median,
    and Mode
The Normal Curve
Skewed Distributions
Bimodal Distributions

Measures of Variation
Range
The Standard Deviation

Measures of Correlation

Using Statistics to Make Predictions
Probability

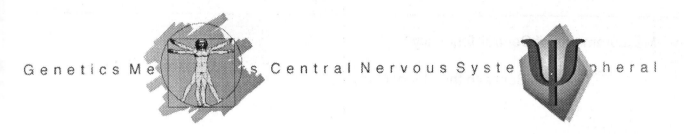
APPENDIX A: MEASURE-MENT AND STATISTICS

Class and Text Notes

This outline provides a way to organize your notes from both the text and the lecture. It will also serve as review sheets for the exam.

Scales of Measurement

    Nominal Scales

    Ordinal Scales

    Interval Scales

    Ratio Scales

Measurements of Central Tendency

Differences Between the Mean, Median, and Mode

The Normal Curve

Skewed Distributions

Bimodal Distributions

Measures of Variation

    Range

    The Standard Deviation

Measures of Correlation

    Scatter plot

    Positive Correlation

    Negative Correlation

Using Statistics to Make Predictions

    Probability

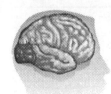

Multiple Choice Posttest

After studying the text and completing the Study Guide activities, answer these questions to determine if you need to review any areas before the course exam.

1. A branch of mathematics that psychologists use to organize and analyze data is known as _____.
   a. calculus
   b. vector analysis
   c. statistics
   d. quantum theory

2. Classifying people according to ethnicity utilizes the _____ scale.
   a. nominal
   b. ordinal
   c. interval
   d. ratio

3. A scale that tells us about order but nothing about the distances between the quantities that are ordered is a(n) _____ scale.
   a. nominal
   b. ordinal
   c. interval
   d. ratio

4. A scale with equal distance between the points, but without a true zero is called a(n) _____scale.
   a. nominal
   b. ordinal
   c. interval
   d. ratio

5. We can say that one measurement is twice as large as another when _____ scales are used.
   a. ordinal
   b. interval
   c. ratio
   d. nominal

6. The auto theft rates of various college campuses is an example of a(n) _____ scale.
   a. nominal
   b. ordinal
   c. interval
   d. ratio

7. The tendency of measurements to cluster around some value near the middle is called the _____.
   a. norm
   b. central tendency
   c. nominal tendency
   d. peripheral tendency

8. Which of the following is NOT a measure of central tendency?
   a. range
   b. mean
   c. median
   d. mode

9. The mean of a set of numbers 30, 40, 43, 88, 10, 20 is _____.
   a. 32
   b. 44
   c. 50
   d. 54

10. A store owner wishes to determine what coat size she should stock in the greatest quantity. She would be most interested in the _____ of her customers' sizes.
    a. range
    b. mean
    c. median
    d. mode

11. A count of the number of scores that fall within different intervals is a(n) _____.
    a. normal curve
    b. frequency distribution
    c. standard deviation
    d. factor analysis

12. In a frequency histogram, frequency is usually marked along the _____.
    a. vertical axis
    b. horizontal axis
    c. diagonal
    d. bar heights

1. c, 2. a, 3. b, 4. c, 5. c, 6. d,
7. b, 8. a, 9. a, 10. d, 11. b, 12. a.